ADVANCE PRAISE

Even in a field as deservedly crowded as Holocaust literature, Kenneth Wald's book is a genuinely singular – and shattering – addition. With an expert scholar's rigor and a family member's emotional stake, he has reassembled the saga of his grandparents and parents from the small town in Germany where they thought themselves fully accepted through the horrors of the Nazi regime, which only the author's mother and father escape. And this is a book not only about the Jews of Germany, but the Christians, as well, both those who betrayed the family and those who have courageously kept alive its memory. *Ghosts on the Wall* is both an interrogation of and an inquiry into history itself.

–Samuel G. Freedman, Professor at Columbia University and author of *Who She Was: My Search for My Mother's Life*

At the heart of this illuminating memoir are Curt and Regina Schönwald, Jewish owners of a textile store in provincial Germany. Murdered in the Holocaust, they live on in their letters to their son in America, in their grandson's efforts to recover their story, and in a few Germans' dedicated memory work. An incisive and deeply moving book.

–Doris Bergin, Chancellor Rose and Ray Wolfe Professor of Holocaust Studies at the University of Toronto and author of *War and Genocide: A Concise History of the Holocaust*

Bringing his impressive scholarly skills to bear on his own family history, the distinguished political scientist Kenneth D. Wald documents the fascinating story of his parents, Jewish refugees from Germany who came to America and established a new life in Lincoln, Nebraska. This is a story not only about persecution and emigration during the Holocaust, but also about life, memory, and identity among Jews in the American heartland in the second half of the 20th century.

–Alan E. Steinweis, University of Vermont

Ken Wald has given us a searching and sensitive account of three generations of his family's history with the Holocaust—and of his evolving views of the nation that perpetrated it. This is a smart, touching, and open-hearted book that deserves a wide readership.

–Peter Hayes, Professor at Northwestern University, author of *Why? Understanding the Holocaust*

THE GHOSTS ON THE WALL

A GRANDSON'S MEMOIR OF THE HOLOCAUST

KENNETH D. WALD

ISBN 9789493322837 (ebook)

ISBN 9789493322820 (paperback)

ISBN 9789493322844 (hardcover)

Publisher: Amsterdam Publishers, The Netherlands

info@amsterdampublishers.com

The Ghosts on the Wall is part of the series Holocaust Survivor True Stories

Copyright © Kenneth D. Wald, 2024

Cover image: Inserted in a depositphotos.com image a photo frame showing Curt and Regina, 1939

All Rights Reserved. No part of this publication may be reproduced or transmitted in any form or by any means, electronic or mechanical, including photocopy, recording or any other information storage and retrieval system, without prior permission in writing from the publisher.

CONTENTS

Preface	xi
Introduction	xiii

PART 1
THE VICTIMS

1. The Letters: Lost and Regained Twice Over	3
2. Meeting the Folks	7
3. The Ghosts on the Wall	12
4. Life in Großröhrsdorf	23

PART 2
THE SURVIVORS

5. Ordeals	41
6. Becoming a Yankee	51
7. My Mother	70
8. Life in Lincoln	89

PART 3
THE AFTERLIFE OF MY GRANDPARENTS

9. Unexpected Voices	103
10. Fruits of Their Labor	115
11. Reckoning: Revenge, Reconciliation, and Responsibility	121
12. On Stage	128
13. Afterlife of the Holocaust	139

Afterword	145
Appendix: The Script of Ghosts on the Wall by Christopher Maly	147
Acknowledgments	177
Photos	181
About the Author	193
Amsterdam Publishers Holocaust Library	195

To Robin, my woman of valor

"The heart has two chambers

Therein live both happiness and pain.

Should happiness awake in one of them,

Then sadness slumbers in the other.

O, Happiness, be careful, speak softly

So that Pain doesn't awake!"

– Inscription by Agnes Schönwald to "my beloved grandson Heinz" (age 11), May 12, 1923, from "The Heart" by Hermann Neumann

---

"There is a way a ghost becomes an ancestor, and traumatic experiences become memories." – **Joseph Bobrow, *Waking Up from War*, 2015**

"...when we tell our parents' tales to the world, or even to ourselves, the story is always our own." – **Scott Turow, *Ordinary Heroes*, 2005**

"Is it possible that the antonym of forgetting is not remembering, but justice?" – **Yosef Hayim Yerushalmi, *Zahor*, 2011**

PREFACE

"Every instant is autonomous. Not vengeance nor pardon nor jails nor even oblivion can modify the invulnerable past." – Jorge Luis Borges, *A New Refutation of Time*

A young prisoner in a Nazi concentration camp described it as a place where "the future is the only certain thing that does not exist."[1] Yet this survivor did have a future after all, living into his 87th year with a family that included a wife, daughter, three grandchildren, and a great-grandson. In the survivor's mind, past, present, and future probably commingled. I suspect his mother and sister, gassed at Auschwitz and Treblinka, respectively, had a seat at the table for holidays and family gatherings.

Though it complicates our understanding of time, the Holocaust has a future. The Shoah did not end after the defeat of Germany but lived on in the memories of survivors who could not forget their parents, siblings, and other victims. In their testimonies, spoken aloud or imagined in silence, they reconstructed the lives of those who perished. Many survivors spent their lives in the shadows cast by that epic trauma long after it receded.

The children of survivors – the successor generation – could not entirely escape their family legacies. Even if they were hazy about the details, most grew up knowing in their bones that something had happened in the distant

---

1. "Otto Dov Kulka, 87, Dies; Studied, and Witnessed, the Holocaust," *New York Times*, March 11, 2021.

past that made their families and relatives "different" and rendered their grandparents present only by their absence.

A generation later, the grandchildren of survivors, removed yet further in time from the genocide, face a world where the renewed threat of fascism once again menaces Jews. After the Nazis swaggered through Charlottesville, Virginia, in 2017, my strong-willed daughter asked tearfully, "Dad, what do I tell the children?" It was a question I never expected to hear. After the 2018 synagogue massacre in Pittsburgh and the US Capitol insurrection in 2021, I imagine many more grandparents and parents heard the same question and, like me, struggled to come up with an answer. Whatever words might have sufficed to explain these events surely failed when trying to make sense of the vicious murders of 1,200 Israelis by Hamas "fighters" late in 2023.

The Passover Haggadah requires Jews to tell the story of the Exodus and retell it in every generation. The story is meant to be conveyed so vividly that all who hear it at the seder table will imagine themselves in Pharaoh's kingdom. They should feel it viscerally, as if they, too, were slaves in Egypt.

Like the annual repetition of the Passover story, relating tales of the Holocaust reminds us that events from the past can defeat time.

We are not done with the Holocaust, and it is not finished with us.

INTRODUCTION

In 2019, I received an extraordinary birthday present from a friend in Germany. Norbert Littig had acquired an embroidered tablecloth from an elderly German lady named Isolde Riss. She told Norbert the tablecloth had been in her family for at least 80 years. At her request, he mailed it to me. I tore open the package, my hands trembling slightly when I felt the fabric.

This was no ordinary piece of linen. It was handed down to Ms. Riss by her father, who worked in the textile store my grandparents owned. The store was the largest commercial building in the German town of Großröhrsdorf, the Schönwald family's home since 1912.

It wasn't just the provenance that mattered. Norbert thought my grandmother Regina had embroidered it. The tablecloth was given to the Riss family in 1938 when my grandparents prepared to depart for a new home in Berlin. Their thriving business, which also housed their residence on the upper floor, had just been stolen by the Nazis in a sham sale to an Aryan businessman. About four years later, my grandparents were exiled to a labor camp in a small Polish town near Lublin. They were presumed murdered in the Sobibor extermination camp in 1943.

Perhaps the story was embroidered just like the tablecloth. I know for certain only that Ms. Riss passed the tablecloth to Norbert, who sent it on to me. His letter makes clear just how tentative any statements about it should be:

The tablecloth is from the Schönwald family. Maybe it was a present for Leonhard Riss, window-dresser, when Curt and Regina went to Berlin in 1938. ... I'm not sure: Maybe the embroidery on the tablecloth is handmade by Regina, your grandmother. Maybe you can see a menorah [a candelabra used in Jewish worship] in a modern style.

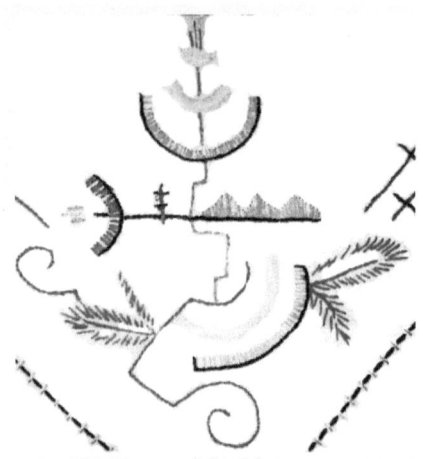

Norbert's musings are plausible. The elderly woman's father definitely worked in my grandparents' textile store. Isolde Riss had previously given me a toy – a yo-yo bearing the store's name and logo. Her father had given it to her when she was a child, her children had played with it, and she said she wanted it restored to its rightful owner. My German-Jewish grandparents, Curt and Regina, surrendered most of their possessions when they were forced out of their spacious home in 1938 – all but what they could carry in two suitcases when they were deported from Germany to Poland in 1942. If they carried any luggage on their way via the Piaski labor camp to Sobibor, I'm sure it was stripped from them and plundered after they were murdered.

The designs in the corners of the tablecloth could be modernistic renderings of a menorah stitched by a Jewish woman. As co-owner of a textile store that catered to seamstresses, my grandmother had access to the necessary materials and probably the skills to decorate the tablecloth. My grandmother, her sister, and my grandfather were deported to Piaski in 1942 – *that* I know for sure – and later to Trawniki, a forced labor camp, and most members of the transport who survived until 1943 were slaughtered in Sobibor later that year.[1]

Whatever its history, I consider the tablecloth a sacred object like a prayer shawl or, perhaps more fittingly, a burial shroud. It is a legacy entrusted to me by a grandmother I never met. I believe that because I want to.

The tablecloth is emblematic of much of the material in this volume. Because this is about family legacies, I cannot be certain of everything I report. I never met my paternal grandparents, my mother didn't know them, and my father did not speak of them. I describe my father's military activity during World War II, but he never wrote a memoir about his war years or told us much about them. He said even less to me about his experiences in Germany after the rise of Hitler. Although I will recount the stories I heard from my mother about her experiences growing up in Germany, her memories were more than 60 years old when she first shared them.

Even apart from the second-hand nature by which I acquired much of the information, I cannot claim that each event or development is retold accurately because memory is inherently emotional and possibly treacherous. People often misremember events in their lives, encase those faulty memories in their brains, and "edit" the memories as time passes. We recall accurately how we felt at the time, our emotional state, but often get the details wrong. In addition to the inherent fallibility of memory, I hadn't planned writing about this odyssey, so I did not keep detailed notes of most conversations and am not always sure how I acquired particular information.

I've tried to confirm my memories by rechecking some encounters also witnessed by my wife, a memory researcher who often recalls things differently than I do. Where possible, I've sought independent corroboration and will identify the sources supporting my claims. For example, I reconstructed many of my father's experiences during World War II from official documents, interviews, and administrative records.

Even though I want to believe what I was told and accept the accuracy of the memories that were shared, there are several instances where I can only surmise or imagine what happened. That's how memoirs work. My standard of proof is not certainty as in a legal proceeding but plausibility and probability. That will have to be enough.

---

1. I obtained my grandparents' deportation certificates to Trawniki. Their likely deportation to Sobibor comes from the Polish Holocaust historian Robert Kuwalek in an email to Norbert Littig, "Re: Transitghetto Piaski," August 10, 2008.

This memoir is an accident. I stumbled onto this topic more because of other people's actions than my own initiative. They led, I followed. This is not false modesty, but simple recognition that the collusion of chance, caprice, and coincidence largely drove me to write this account.

This is not really my memoir even though I recount some personal incidents and experiences. It is a memoir mostly of those who experienced the Holocaust before I was born – my parents and grandparents, in particular. Because the story is told through my voice and extends to the present day, I am not absent from the text but am mostly a vehicle for transmitting what happened to other members of my family. Although I use their words, the perspectives are mine alone.

As a child growing up in a modest home at 2764 South 33rd Street in Lincoln, Nebraska, I often sat at our dining room table facing the wall hung with a portrait of my paternal grandparents. That's when I first thought of them as ghosts, and so the phrase "ghosts on the wall" embedded itself in my memory. In time, I broadened my efforts to understand my ancestors by incorporating the experiences of my mother's family and my parents. All of them are gone now, their photographs gracing the ancestor wall at our home in Gainesville, Florida. More than 1,300 miles away from Lincoln, the very same portrait of Curt and Regina that once stared at me as a child now nests comfortably among the extended family of specters that has grown well beyond my grandparents.

Coincidences have played a huge role in this story. Crime investigators consider coincidences as clues that help solve mysteries. Theologians and believers often think that chance occurrences represent fate, the working of God's will. Even people who are not religious may suppose that things happen for a reason, that the universe has a purpose for each of us.

As someone who was taught the law of large numbers, I know that seemingly random events with extremely low probabilities happen in due course and require no supernatural assistance. As a rationalist, I am uncomfortable with mystical claims that the universe wants something to take place for its own mysterious reasons. Nonetheless, the haphazard and unplanned series of discoveries that I stumbled upon provided clues that solved family mysteries, linked me to my ancestors, and now led me to tell their stories. As hard as it is to admit, I want to believe it was no coincidence.

PART 1
THE VICTIMS

1 THE LETTERS: LOST AND REGAINED TWICE OVER

A disordered pile of yellowing papers first drew me into my family's encounter with the Holocaust.[1] After my father died in 1986, my brother Steve and I met at my parents' condo in the Wellington Greens subdivision of Lincoln, our hometown. He and I went to search my father's small basement office, hunting for documents needed to settle his estate. Apart from learning that he hid a lot of traffic tickets that we would have teased him about mercilessly had we known about them, there wasn't much to pique our interest. However, while pulling files from a drawer, I found one old, fat, faded manila folder that changed everything.

The documents crammed inside were mostly typewritten on aged, crumbly stationery. I could make out the dates – mostly in the 1940s – and recognized they were in German. Having grown up hating anything related to Germany, a country that brutalized my parents, Heinz (later Henry in the United States) and Margaret (Gretl), and killed my relatives, neither my brother nor I read or spoke the accursed language. But I had unwittingly picked up just enough kitchen-table German to recognize that the papers were letters to my father from his parents in Germany. The clue was the salutation, "*Lieber Heinz* [Dear Heinz]." They were mailed to him first in

---

1. The letters are now housed at the Price Library of Judaica at the University of Florida's Smathers Library in Gainesville. The collection is catalogued as Schönwald Family Correspondence and a finding aid is available at https://findingaids.uflib.ufl.edu/repositories/2/resources/1582.

New York, where he had arrived in March 1939, and then to wherever he moved around the country before settling in Lincoln.

The letters were the first items touched by my grandparents that I'd ever held in my hands. My grandparents had been living in a "Jews House" in Berlin since late 1938 when the Nazis stole their department store.

I knew almost nothing about them except that they had, as my mother put it, "died in the war." My father said virtually nothing about them to any of us. My mother, who also left Germany without her family in 1939, never met her in-laws. In the photo on the wall, they looked stiff, very serious, and I felt no connection to them whatsoever. Because they were never talked about, they seemed lifeless. They were related to my father but not connected to me. They were ghosts who didn't haunt me.

Growing up with no grandparents, I thought my family history began in 1939 when my parents arrived in the United States as refugees from Nazi Germany. The few relatives whom the Holocaust didn't eliminate lived in southern Africa and New York – places that might as well have been on the other side of the moon from my perch in Nebraska.[2] If we'd ever hosted a family reunion, we would all have fit comfortably inside a telephone booth.

Finding the trove of letters in 1986 taught me that I wasn't as alone as I'd imagined. I knew I had discovered something important but not why it mattered. I asked my mother if she wanted to read the letters before I took them home to Florida. She said yes. Every time I returned to Nebraska to visit her, I would pull out the file and page through the letters, knowing they were important but not what I would do with them.

My mother eventually moved from the condo she had shared with my father to an apartment in a senior living facility grandly named "Van Dorn Villas." Because of teaching responsibilities, I couldn't help with the move but told my brother to make sure the letters were safely transported to the new residence. On subsequent visits to her new home, I found the letters on a shelf and sorted through them aimlessly. Whenever I asked her if I could finally hold onto them, she said she planned to read them but hadn't gotten around to it yet. During one visit, I couldn't find them on the shelf and she didn't recall where she'd moved them. It was a short trip and I didn't have

---

2. I met my Aunt Suse when she came to Lincoln for my bar mitzvah in 1962. Lincoln was a small enough city and South Africa sufficiently exotic to warrant a story about the visit in the local newspaper. "Brother, Sister Meet After 23 Year Separation," *Lincoln Journal-Star*, May 22, 1962.

time to search the apartment thoroughly, figuring I'd find them the next time I came to town. She died before I could return for that next visit.

After my mother died in 2000, the family got together to apportion her belongings. My mother had always told me that she worried my brother and I would fight over her things after her death. I asked Mom why she didn't avoid this feared outcome by making her wishes known in writing, but she insisted we would work it out ourselves after she was gone. She hated making decisions, so I didn't confront her about it.

My wife, Robin, later told me that what she really worried about was that her two daughters-in-law would feud about the ownership of her jewelry, which they split up without rancor in about five minutes. Her fears about Steve and me came true as we did fight over her belongings, albeit not quite the way she had imagined.

Me: "I don't want that. You take it."

Steve: "No, I've already got one of those, so it's yours."

Me: "It won't fit in my house."

Steve: "I'll never use it."

All the adults (in unison): "Let's give it to the kids."

All the kids (in unison): "We don't want it, either."

Exhausted from trying to palm off unwanted items on one another, we sat around the coffee table in the living room.

My priority was to locate the letters from my grandparents, the only thing I really wanted other than the pressure cooker, which I associated with my mother's wonderful sauerkraut. Despite a thorough search, we couldn't find the folder I'd discovered 14 years earlier. I despaired that the letters had not survived, that she had thrown them away after finally reading them, or absent-mindedly put them in a pile of papers that went into the trash.

The more I thought about it, the more frustrated and angry I became. Finally, I slammed my fist down on the arm of my chair. My outburst ignited a tremor that traveled a short distance across the floor, reaching a battered old ottoman nearby with just enough force to briefly pop open the lid. We'd used that ancient piece of furniture as a footrest and I'd forgotten that it had a storage compartment. I opened it up, dug down under a pile of old blankets, and found the folder with the treasured letters intact. With nobody else claiming it, I became the unofficial caretaker and took the letters home to Florida for safekeeping.

2 MEETING THE FOLKS

In one of many coincidences that may not have been coincidences, I was scheduled to join a study tour in Germany in the summer of 2000, shortly after my mother's death. I was motivated to join this tour by the opportunity to meet Holocaust scholars who could contribute to the University of Florida's Center for Jewish Studies, which I then directed. Since I was going to be in Germany, I decided to visit my father's hometown of Großröhrsdorf, a small city just a few kilometers outside Dresden in the state of Saxony, before the tour began. I wrote down my paternal grandparents' Berlin apartment address, thinking I might have time to locate the building where the letters were written before their deportation.

In Berlin, I found my way to No. 10/11 Kolonnstrasse in the Schöneberg neighborhood, my grandparents' last address in Germany. I was mildly surprised to find the building undamaged but even more shocked by the impact of locating it. As I stood just outside the doorway of what had been the "Jews House," the Schönwalds' last real home, I felt a glimmer of a connection to my grandparents and found myself silently reciting the Kaddish, the traditional Jewish mourning prayer. I touched the public mailbox just outside the entrance, hoping it had once held the letters to my father from my grandparents.

Even in this freewheeling, cosmopolitan area of Berlin, home today to crossdressers and numerous nonconformists of various stripes, passersby gave a wide berth to the middle-aged man with one hand on the post box, the other atop his head in place of a *yarmulke* (Jewish head covering), his lips moving without making sounds, and barely discernible tears in his eyes. No one who saw this strange sight was more surprised by my behavior than me.

In the old Jewish quarter of Berlin, I found a train track that carried many of the city's Jews – probably including my grandparents – to their deaths in the East. A monument on the platform was covered with stones – it is a Jewish custom for mourners to leave a stone to show they had visited a gravesite. Even though this was not a grave, the homage struck me as perfect because most of those long-gone deportees have no grave to hold their bones and no headstone to proclaim: "I was here; my life mattered." I added a small rock to the collection atop the monument.

During the subsequent study tour across Germany, I could not stop talking about my grandparents. When I returned to Berlin at the end of the tour, I recited the Kaddish at the weekly Sabbath service in a nearby synagogue. I stood while reciting it, as is the custom, announcing to the congregants my bereavement at my mother's recent death but also in tribute to my grandparents. Because nearly 80 years had passed since my grandparents died, I have since tried to make up for the years when they were not part of my life by reciting their names whenever I say the mourning prayer.

The short trip to Großröhrsdorf in what was formerly communist East Germany was even more compelling. My grandparents lived there for 30-plus years, producing two children – my father Heinz and his sister Suse (pronounced Sooza) – and building a successful business that was expanded two times. My host, Markus Nitsche, was the grandson of a man with whom my father had corresponded in the 1980s. Before leaving the United States for this trip, I had written to Markus's grandfather, Reinhard Gebler, to suggest a meeting. I did not know that he had since died. Fortunately, Markus answered the letter and arranged the visit for my wife and me.

Markus was very close to his grandfather. A young law student when I first met him at Tegel Airport in Berlin, Markus told me that *Herr* Gebler had kept a hidden archive of my family during both the Nazi and communist periods, a cache that could have gotten him into trouble with both regimes. The photos, documents, and newspaper articles that his grandfather had collected were hidden in the stovepipe of his apartment. Markus told me that his grandfather often reminisced about the Schönwalds and entrusted the records to him.

We began with a courtesy visit to the mayor, a holdover from the days of communism, and I saw my grandparents' store among the guilds and businesses painted on a mural of town history. That was the first sign that the Schönwalds were not entirely absent from Großröhrsdorf despite their physical departure 60 years earlier. While Markus was showing us around the town, we stopped in a churchyard where he greeted an older man, Kurt Schossig. The man said he remembered our family. They were aristocrats, he said, high-society folks, but went on to tell us of their public-mindedness.

He told about an incident when a factory worker in town was seriously injured in an industrial accident. When his fellow workers begged the factory owner to drive the man to nearby Dresden where his life-threatening injuries could be treated, he refused, fearing the man would bleed all over his car. So they went to my grandfather, who had no relationship to the factory or the worker but did have a car. He drove the injured man 39 km (24 miles) to Dresden. Another time, he insisted on driving home a female customer in the family store who was in the advanced stages of pregnancy.

We interrupted the tour to eat lunch at the Ratskeller in the Großröhrsdorf town hall. The restaurant was crowded with a large group attending a school reunion. One of the attendees approached me and said she had heard that descendants of Curt and Regina Schönwald were visiting. She recognized me instantly because she said I looked just like my grandfather.

Her comment took me aback. I vaguely recall my father occasionally pointing out my resemblance to my grandfather but had not realized how much we looked alike. There had been talk of naming me after him, but it was dropped because they probably didn't want to give me a German name. When I was five years old, my father wrote to his sister that "Kenny looks more and more like his grandfather on my side," so this was not the first time somebody saw my grandfather in me. He went on to describe me at the age of five as "a very short-tempered guy" who "gets fits of anger, screams and yells ..." He called me "a real Tobias," which I'm told is not a compliment. I'm sure he confused me with my brother or his younger self.

The woman in the Ratskeller, Ilse Knösch, went on to tell me she had been friendly with the Schönwalds. In fact, she had exchanged letters with my grandmother when they were in Berlin, but her letters eventually stopped and the woman's letters to my grandmother were returned. She asked me what had become of them.

I hadn't been reluctant to tell people about my grandparents' fate, but this was the first time I encountered an acquaintance who did not know how the story ended. She was saddened when I told her. I said I was very interested in anything my grandmother might have written to her and we exchanged addresses. She later wrote from her home in Maintal that she could not find any correspondence but did attach a small photo of my grandparents – a print of the same portrait on the dining room wall of my childhood home in Lincoln. She believed it was a farewell present from my grandmother after they left Großröhrsdorf for Berlin.

Thanks to the stories Markus recounted and chance meetings with older townspeople, my grandparents had begun to edge their way back into my life. On my return to Florida, I hired a German graduate student who lovingly translated their letters into English.

When I first discovered the letters years before, I noticed that each had a number based on the date my grandparents had written it. Somehow they had gotten out of numerical order. Almost without thinking, I immediately sorted them by date.[1] Once I had them in chronological order, I glanced at the German text and then read the English translation.

I never anticipated that reading the letters would make me feel close to my ancestors, but as I paged through their correspondence, it happened. In one of the first letters, my grandfather insisted that my father, too, should number and date his letters to the family in Germany. Because letters often arrived out of order and were not dated, the parents otherwise could not be sure if he had received their letters. The son must not have acted on this appeal immediately because his father kept repeating the request. From that demand, I learned that I resembled my grandfather not only in physical features but also in a certain degree of compulsiveness. I imagined him with a smile on his face as his diligent grandson brought chronological order to the large pile of letters without having been asked.

In the third letter, my grandmother wrote a few lines to raise my father's morale after he expressed frustration about his job prospects in New York. Radiating warmth in her concern for her son, I realized that she was not the cold, distant parent that my own mother had surmised. As irrational as it was, I felt comforted by my grandfather's approval and my grandmother's generous emotional support.

When this odyssey began, I had no direct experience with grandparents. My mother's parents had died of natural causes before my birth. My parents were loving but not very demonstrative and my father regarded self-

---

1. The letters were translated by Margit Grieb, now a professor in the Department of World Languages at the University of South Florida in Tampa.

esteem as a disease that needed to be cured rather than a trait to be encouraged. Praise came sparingly, if at all. Perhaps he was imitating the behavior of his grandmother, a powerful and independent-minded woman who probably was not much for sentimentality.

As a teenager, I realized how little I knew about the bond between grandparents and grandkids when I talked to a friend whose grandfather had recently died. Trying to empathize, I told him with absolute sincerity that I understood his grief because my beloved dog had just died, too. His anger told me just how clueless I was about the rich emotions that develop between grandparents and grandchildren. Because I did not get to experience that relationship as a child, becoming a grandfather four times over has been especially sweet.

When I returned home after visiting Großröhrsdorf in 2000, I called my brother, eager to tell him the wonderful stories about our grandparents. Almost immediately, we ran into a communication problem. We had no language to identify the objects of our conversation. "Grandfather" and "Grandmother" were titles we had never used for anybody in our lives. Using "Mr. and Mrs. Schönwald" was ridiculously formal, while "Curt and Regina" seemed too intimate for people we had never met. After several pauses, we settled on the awkward impersonal phrases "Dad's dad" and "Dad's mom."

Although I felt a growing connection to them, it was still unformed. Only after reading the letters did I discover that I had grandparents, that I was a grandson for real. I processed my feelings by writing about them. My first essay, "The Ghosts on the Wall," was meant to describe what it was like to meet my grandparents when I was middle-aged, when they first became real to me.[2] I reproduce it with minimal editing in the next chapter.

---

2. The article appeared in *Midstream* 54.2 (March/April 2008), 18–22.

3   THE GHOSTS ON THE WALL

I grew up in a house full of ghosts. The spirits were not formless apparitions floating from room to room but strong images in elegantly framed photographs, tethered firmly to the dining room wall by history and memory as much as by wire and hook. Posed formally in the fashion of their day, stiff and unsmiling, they did not haunt me. Because of their vast distance from my life, they were my father's parents, not in any sense my grandparents. They were flesh but not blood.

All that began to change years later on a sunny spring afternoon as I stood in the kitchen of my Florida home, leafing through a bulging folder rescued from my father's files after his death. The folder held almost 200 letters and notes his parents had sent to him from Germany in the late 1930s and early 1940s. Faced with a disordered pile of papers written in German, a language I was proud *not* to read, I sorted idly through the mound of yellowing documents.

I had never asked my father about his parents because my mother had warned me that such questions would reopen old wounds. Even so, a few things had slipped out over the years. His parents, Curt and Regina Schönwald, were native-born Germans, descended from a family with Prussian roots going back to the 18th century. A patriotic German, my grandfather served with distinction in the Kaiser's air force during World War I, rising to the rank of squad commander and, it was said, supervising a young pilot named Hermann Göring who later became commander of the German Air Force in World War II.[1]

In 1912, my grandparents moved from Berlin to Großröhrsdorf, They were dry goods merchants with a small but prosperous textile store. They were the only Jews in town. Having a bar mitzvah in the Dresden Synagogue, educated in the local high school, my father later attended the Institute of Technology in that city (where the celebrated diarist Victor Klemperer taught) and worked in his parents' store.

In January 1933, Adolf Hitler was appointed chancellor of Germany and seized emergency powers two months later, ending Germany's postwar democratic experiment. In short order, civil liberties were curtailed severely, the *Reichstag* [German parliament] reduced to a Nazi puppet, anti-Jewish riots instigated across the country, and a network of concentration camps established to house dissidents, communists, and other political prisoners. After five years of increasing repression, a policy of random harassment and persecution evolved into a systematic plan to isolate and then drive out the Jews of Germany.

The plan was baptized by the *Kristallnacht* [Night of Broken Glass] pogrom in November 1938. This supposed "spontaneous" demonstration of anger against Jews was a well-planned and choreographed race riot directed by the local Nazi cadres who marched on synagogues and Jewish businesses, setting fire to those buildings that could be burned to the ground without damaging Aryan property. The rioters took special pleasure in throwing rocks through the windows of Jewish-owned businesses and painting vile slogans on the walls. In Großröhrsdorf, the church bells summoned a mob that followed the script by shattering the windows and painting a swastika on the Kaufhaus Schönwald, the family's department store. My father and grandfather were arrested, deported to Buchenwald, and released two months later.

As the rising tide of antisemitism closed in on the Schönwald family, the first priority was to save the children. My father was old enough to leave the country on his own. He managed somehow to get out of Germany in 1939, coming to the United States via Switzerland and England. His sister Suse fled with her husband to the Netherlands, a way station en route to their eventual destination of Rhodesia (now Zimbabwe) in southern Africa. After their business and home were stolen from them, my grandparents moved back to Berlin.

---

1. Subsequent research by Norbert Littig, my German friend, cast doubt on this claim.

That was as much of the story as I knew. Of my grandparents, I knew only that, to quote my mother's refrain whenever I asked about any of our relatives, "They died in the war." Although nothing was ever said, I understood clearly enough they were not warriors or Resistance fighters – heroic figures firing on Nazi convoys from ambushes, throwing hand grenades during pitched street battles with the SS. In my young mind, if they could not be heroes, they were nothing, people defined more by their absence from my life than their presence in another time. As I got older, it became easier to imagine them as a respectable, sedate couple in late middle age, forced into premature retirement by the Nazi seizure of their store in 1939. Bereft of children, isolated, harassed, and threatened daily, it must have felt as if the walls were closing in on them. I pictured them sinking into torpor, surrendering to their ordained fate as Holocaust victims.

Just a few letters into the musty stack of documents on my kitchen counter, something happened that shattered my image of their fatalism. I came across a letter written in April 1939, when my father was already in New York and his parents were settled in Berlin. My grandmother suddenly switched to English to describe their situation in Berlin. She chose English, I believe, to help her son gain fluency in his new environment and to refresh her language skills in preparation for eventual relocation to the United States.

> I would like to correspond with you in English, you must of course write German so that Father ["*Vatel*"] can read it himself. Your letter I have read many times, for god's sake don't lose hope ... Think [of] ... the Easter week last year, then enjoy everything [that] comes across your way. Father and I take our long walks and we enjoy it very much, we have beautiful spring days. On holidays and Sundays we walk in the forenoon, on other days in the afternoon. Very often we meet Uncle & Aunt and we see the old Berlin – trees and old parks that we knew 35 years ago. Our flat is now very nice and so comfortable. Everything has found a place and the nice furniture is also very practical.
>
> With fondest care to you and all relations, a kiss, my dear boy.

In my Holocaust-decimated household, that moment of contact across the generations counted as a family reunion. With a brief message intended only to cheer up her son, my grandmother dispelled my notion that she and my grandfather had given up on life as the Nazi regime pressed down on them.

As the set of letters revealed, they did not stop living even as their world turned upside down. Who would have blamed them if they had succumbed to despair as a poisonous set of laws reduced them to the servile status of nonpersons? Within months of Kristallnacht, Jews were banned from sports grounds, public baths, parks, swimming pools, theaters, cinemas, libraries, concerts, exhibitions, and music halls. Soon, they would be ordered to surrender radios, typewriters, telephones, and house pets, and forbidden to purchase tobacco or flowers. In a blend of martial law and house arrest that amounted to internal exile, local officials could proscribe Jews from certain areas and order them off the streets at will.

One would not know any of that from the restrained letters sent to my father in New York by his parents in Berlin. No doubt mindful of the censor and not wanting to distress their son, they betrayed only oblique references to the aftermath of Kristallnacht, the confiscation of their store in 1939, or the other humiliations visited on them daily. There is no self-pity in these remarkably forbearing accounts of daily life. As shopkeepers rather than intellectuals, social critics, or journalists, they resolutely avoided the big picture and simply told their son what they were doing.

There was not always a lot to tell. While my grandmother assured her son that "we are doing something all the time," my grandfather confessed with remarkable understatement, "we don't have many diversions here." From time to time, the reality of Nazi restrictions on Jews broke through the otherwise even tone. "I sometimes long to have a shop again," my grandmother wrote late in 1939, less than a year after the "Law for the Exclusion of Jews from German Economic Life" prohibited such activity. My grandfather dreamed in April 1940 about how wonderful it would be to drive a car again. That was only a dream because the Reich had confiscated driver's licenses from Jews two years earlier.

My grandparents betrayed emotion only when their children's welfare was concerned. As Suse prepared to leave Germany, my grandmother aptly characterized her mixed feelings. "We are witnessing this," she wrote of Suse's impending departure on May 25, 1939, "with one laughing and one crying eye." Still, she told him, their safety was paramount. "I am so happy when I think of you all and how you are mastering your situations," she wrote to both her children in July 1940. "It would be too good to be true to think of a reunion but I still hope for it." As my grandfather affirmed four months later, "The only wish your mother and I still have is to be able to be together with you. Hopefully, we will live to see the day."

Rather than ruminate on their fate, my grandparents filled their letters to my father with warmth and emotional support as he navigated alone through a strange new world. If they could not be there to help him, there was no shortage of advice about how to get a job, plan a career, find a suitable wife, placate a boss. The comments even extended to matters of personal hygiene. Praising him for taking good care of his clothing, my grandmother could not help but ask, "Are you keeping your comb and brush clean?" Apparently not happy with the answer, she teased him a month later: "Are you keeping your comb and brush clean, or do I have to come and check up on you?" As soon as my father landed a plum job as a salesclerk in August 1939, he was told by his doting mother to take care of his feet and admonished by both parents to show "his European side" by displaying exquisite politeness even if that was not the usual practice in a partially civilized country. When the nearly 30-year-old bristled at all this helpful advice from a distance in a letter at the end of 1940, his father responded in kind: "Even though you are over 17 years old, as you reminded us in your last letter, that doesn't mean that your Mother stops worrying about you!" Neither, I suspect, did his father.

My father's adventures with various young ladies occasioned comment from both parents. When he learned that my father was dating several women at once in June 1941, my grandfather advised him "to get a register for all of your flames so that you don't get the different dates mixed up" and likened him to the family's notoriously womanizing (and aptly named) Uncle Lothar. One of my father's first jobs was to light the boiler in a girls' dormitory at the local university. On hearing of the successful repair of the broken furnace in December 1940, his mother slyly congratulated him for "heating up those young ladies again." On a more serious note, when the young man confided difficulties with a woman whom he wanted to marry, his mother shared his pain. "There's nothing I want more for you than a lovely wife who feels for you and understands you and shares life with you," she wrote. Eager to be of help, she implored him to keep her informed. "I don't want to jump ahead and wait for your next letter," she prodded him in April 1940. "There is still much that a mother has to say in such a situation." She proceeded to prove it with a stream of advice, commiseration, and encouragement from what she called "my silly mother heart."

The general tone of the Schönwald letters from 1939 to 1940 is not upbeat to be sure but is better described as hopeful and, in a way, defiant. My grandparents looked forward to the next phase of their life, the time when they could join my father in the United States. They asked his advice about how best to equip themselves for a productive life in America. Just a month after my father arrived in the United States in March 1939, my grandmother asked him whether she should concentrate on "cooking and baking, or flowers, or sewing aprons," while my grandfather, who had been a distillery apprentice in his youth, vowed to refresh his knowledge of liqueur production if his son thought it would be useful after emigration. My father must have encouraged him because my grandfather reported in early July: "I'm now attending a distillery course, and things are slowly coming back to me." There was some false modesty in this brief report as my grandmother noted with pride: "Everybody receives homemade eggnog from Father now and they all love it."

My grandmother similarly threw herself into self-improvement. "I go to our cooking course every afternoon, almost the whole day," she told her son in June 1939. "I am learning a lot of new things, and hopefully I will be able to use it someday. I have really perfected my cooking skills. It's serious business for me now when the pots hit the table." To prove the point again, and in an oblique reference to my grandfather's imprisonment in Buchenwald, she added: "Father is gaining weight again and looks a lot healthier." My grandfather readily agreed, telling his son that his mother cooked "fabulously" and, Jewish mother that she was, regretted "she wasn't able to cook this well when you were still here." Not content with improving her general kitchen skills, she wanted to do more, asking her son in June 1941 about the advisability of learning to prepare salads and praliné. She also added baking to her portfolio, assuring my father in February 1941 that "I'll be able to earn a little on the side that way."

Thinking that food service was a good career option when they reached the United States, my grandfather also took the plunge in January 1940, enrolling in a confectionary class with five women he playfully described as his harem. After completing a second course in July, he could proudly report to his son: "I am a professional confectionary maker now." Once in the United States, he suggested, they could join forces in a catering operation "where I can brew the liqueurs and fruit juices and Mother will prepare the salads and sandwiches." If that didn't work out, my grandfather suggested, perhaps they could go together in the grocery business. "I would be glad," he told his son, "if you could open a small store selling groceries. It's better to be modestly self-employed than working for someone else." Alluding both to his current straits and my father's previous employment in the family textile store, my grandfather admitted: "Unfortunately I cannot aid you financially; I would love to help you out. Maybe one day I can work for you nonetheless, like you did for me."

This correspondence occurred amid the passage of compulsory labor laws that forced Jews to work for the *Reich*, the slamming shut of gates to Jewish refugees around the world, the German invasion of Poland, and an event not even mentioned in the correspondence, the outbreak of war pitting Germany against Britain and France. I do not think my grandparents were oblivious. Despite censorship, as Klemperer's celebrated diaries revealed, word about what was happening did get back by stealth to German Jews. The letters report the desperate circumstances of relatives, friends, and acquaintances, including a suicide, which was not uncommon among German Jews after Hitler came to power in 1933. Recognizing they could do nothing about the situation at large, my grandparents worked assiduously on what they could control, their preparation for a new life in America.

In learning English, my grandmother outpaced my grandfather. Shortly after my father left Germany in 1939, she proudly informed him that she had begun language study by participating in a conversational circle that involved speaking, translation, debate, and dictation. Having spoken English as a little girl, she was confident enough to assess her classmates. "The participants all speak very well," she judged, "but I think that they have bad pronunciation." By October 1940, radiating confidence, she boasted: "I'm really doing well now in American conversation. I'm also enjoying … American books." She told him about learning "popular expressions like *flu* for a cold" and mastering idioms and other practical things. Yet despite her pride in "learning to speak in the American way," progress was slow. Recognizing the difficulty of mastering a new culture at their ages, she admitted to her son late in June 1940, "It will be difficult for us, and we will probably always stay the same behind our own four walls."

Whatever happened, both parents assured their son they would take any work that came their way. When my father complained about having to start over in yet another trade in August 1939, my grandfather reminded him of his own experience: "Just imagine, I started out in a distillery and moved to distribution, then changed to a spirit and yeast factory, then to a mill, back to the distillery, then sold greeting cards, changed to being a traveling salesman for cigar-holders, and then carpets, and finally became a textile merchant. As you can see, I changed my careers eight times and never lost courage."

If the best they could find in America was minimum wage work with long hours, my grandfather assured his son in the same letter, that was no problem. "Mother... [and] I would love to work with you, even if it were 15 hours a day," he declared, and my grandmother confirmed to him at the end of January 1941 that "you can count on your parents when it comes to working hard." She assured him they would not become a burden in the United States: "I am well conditioned by my housework, so that I can work in any household and do just about any job there. I've always held the belief that no type of work is degrading, even the most undignified chores."

At worst, they would simply make him a good home. "When we're living with you and you have to work so much," his mother promised, "you'll be able to come home to find a comfortable space. I'm longing so much for the opportunity to do everything for you. You've really earned it."

In April 1940, my grandfather declared rather casually, "We will have to think about emigration soon." The low-key tone was apparently meant to disguise some urgency because, just a year earlier, my grandfather had announced a three-year extension of their apartment lease. Perhaps he had heard the rumors from Eastern Europe about the mass deportations of Jews and the mobile killing squads that followed the German war machine as it swept across Poland. The impulse to leave could have arisen from something closer to home: cuts in pensions and food rations for Jews, new and confiscatory tax levies, or, more ominously, the first German efforts to gas the mentally handicapped that had begun in 1939. Whatever the source, my grandparents now devoted their time to identifying options, making plans, and tracking down and evaluating every possibility.

For almost two years, they explored every potential lifeline no matter how remote it seemed. Although Shanghai, Santo Domingo, and Africa were explored as possible destinations, my grandparents concentrated on obtaining visas to join their son in the United States. That decision thrust them into a labyrinthine American immigration process made even more feckless by the war. They became subject to a world where something as trivial as a delay in mailing a package or a misplaced signature could set the process back by months or years. "Please don't think that my requests are unfounded and based on my imagination," my grandfather assured his son in June 1941, "... rather [they are] drawn from experiences with acquaintances whose efforts have all in one way or another failed, whether due to missing or falsely sent documents." In this anxious if not Kafkaesque atmosphere, talk of affidavits, security deposits, financial guarantees, quotas, and case numbers increasingly dominated the correspondence.

Members of the stern, self-reliant bourgeoisie, it was painful for my grandparents to press their needs upon their distant son. The letters reverberate with expressions of confidence in my father's efforts and mortification that their plight wore him down. At the end of September 1941, my grandfather spoke of "my bad conscience that you may get yourself into deep financial troubles in order to help us." If something so insubstantial as money weighed on his mind, how he must have anguished over telling his son in October 1941 that his marriage to an American citizen would enhance their chances of securing a visa or advising him to forego a business opportunity because a move to a small town in Wyoming ("in Indian territory") would delay their correspondence. "This all may sound egotistical," he admitted, "but you can believe me when I tell you that our move has reached a point where every day could make a difference."

Two of my father's romances apparently collapsed under the pressure. As my grandfather ruefully told his son in February 1941,

> "We've always known that you would be there for us if we ever needed your help, but you did even more. You've given up a girl for our sake. We cannot express our appreciation with a few words. What we feel is a deep and heartfelt gratitude. We will do anything within our powers to pay off our debt to you, I'll promise you that and will keep my word."

My grandmother, who normally left talk about immigration matters to her husband, weighed in with some motherly advice in the same February letter:

> "we are both feeling so lucky to have such a wonderful child [as] you. We feel incredible joy. We also feel a little bit bad that you had to give up your girl who meant so much to you, and mostly because of us. It is *impossible* for her to care as much for our fate as you may have asked her to do."

Based on their quota number and the materials my father had marshaled on their behalf, my grandparents expected to board a ship to America by the spring or summer of 1941. As the season neared, they badgered my father for advice about the specifics of the trip. My grandfather noted that the cost of shipping furniture was prohibitive, and they would send only clothing and housewares. "Do we need featherbeds over there?" he asked, "or are our down comforters enough?" My grandmother wondered about bringing electrical appliances like the vacuum cleaner and toaster.

Their chances to board a ship to the United States diminished greatly on June 19, 1941. Responding to the expulsion of German diplomatic personnel from the United States, the Reich closed American consular offices in Germany. With that decision, my grandparents lost any prospect of securing the necessary visas quickly. As my grandfather admitted in an August letter, "Our chances for relocation are slim [but] we are still going to continue to hope for the best." He was philosophical about the delay. "We can't fight the facts," my grandfather counseled his disappointed son, "and simply have to deal with things as they are. There's no sense in crying about it, that won't change anything and just depresses everybody involved."

They began to explore a more complicated plan involving a tourist visa to Cuba. About seven months later, on November 22, 1941, my grandfather wrote with good news. Thanks to my father's hard work, they had secured immigration authorization to Cuba, a way station before an eventual landing in the United States. As soon as their new passports arrived, they would book passage. A worried son could now finally relax and accept his father's heartfelt thanks for all his sacrifices. It looked as though the story would have a happy ending.

As far as I know, that was the last communication my father ever received from his parents. They had been waiting patiently for the new passports required to leave Germany. Unknown to them, the Reich had stopped issuing passports to Jews, reflecting the 1941 change in policy from expulsion to extermination.[2] They were trapped. For a brief time, my grandfather was ordered to work as a slave laborer in a Berlin electrical factory. A Gestapo memorandum dated March 28, 1942, reports that Curt and Regina Schönwald (deportees 10326 and 10327, respectively) were transported by train to Trawniki labor camp near Lublin in Poland. The *Gedenkbuch*, a postwar memorial book that documented the fate of

---

2. The best source on Germany's decision to exterminate the Jews is Christopher P. Browning, *The Origins of the Final Solution* (Lincoln, NE: University of Nebraska Press, 2004), chapters 8–9.

German Jews under National Socialism, confirms the transport but is silent about what happened next to my father's parents. The *Encyclopedia of the Holocaust* notes that many Trawniki inmates died of starvation and disease while others were sent to the Belzec death camp for extermination. Possibly, they were among the 10,000 Jewish inmates of Trawniki shot on November 5, 1943, following an uprising in Sobibor. For bureaucratic reasons, my grandparents' official date of death was May 12, 1945, the day the war ended – and my father's birthday. Perhaps to rid himself of his ghosts, he insisted that I become a bar mitzvah on the same day 17 years later.

Through these letters, those ghosts in the photographs that hung on the wall of my childhood home have shed their spectral cloak and assumed human dimensions. My grandparents have reached out to me across time, space, and memory. For all the details, the most important thing I've learned is that they did not surrender in the face of crushing reality. They did not join the Resistance, but Curt and Regina resisted by refusing to shout lamentations or succumb to despair, by the heroic act of imagining and planning a life for themselves in the New World. My grandparents never got the chance to live that life, except vicariously, but the vision sustained them in the darkest moments. I was wrong when I assumed they were led meekly as sheep to the slaughter. I know now that my mother was wrong when she said they "died in the war." As I learned from their testament, my grandparents died *fighting* the war.

4 LIFE IN GROSSRÖHRSDORF

The letters my grandparents wrote to my father were sent from Berlin, the town where both had been born and spent their early lives. Of Großröhrsdorf, the letters said little. They did not discuss losing their home and business with my father, who had lived with them, but it left a gaping hole in my understanding of life before Hitler. Knowing nothing about what they experienced, I imagined that their life in Großröhrsdorf was hellish from beginning to end (1912–1938). That assumption flowed easily from my "lifetime of aversion therapy against the country" and led to a consuming hatred of all things Germanic.[1]

Although my parents occasionally let slip a sentimental thought about their homeland, I considered myself an American entirely free of German traits. I rooted enthusiastically against German teams in the Olympics, flashed a dirty look at anybody speaking German in my presence, and celebrated Germany's forcible partition after World War II. As a self-proclaimed Germanophobe, I considered its 1990 reunification a tragedy that should be undone. When people from the former East Germany tried to explain to me that they, too, had suffered during World War II and then under decades of communist rule, I was tempted to ask them how many of their grandparents had been murdered.

The collapse of the Soviet Union led to an exodus of Russian Jews after

---

1. Edie Jarolim, "Vienna Calling," *Tablet*, March 3, 2022, https://www.tabletmag.com/sections/community/articles/vienna-calling-austrian-citizenship.

1989. Preferring a more European environment than they could find in North America, a significant portion moved to Germany. I found the very idea of Jews returning to Germany voluntarily simply incomprehensible if not obscene. One of my fellow participants on a Fulbright study tour in 2000 told me that her Jewish grandparents, converts to Christianity, had returned to Germany after World War II when her grandfather resumed his position as a judge. She said they considered the Holocaust a tragedy but it had nothing to do with them. Tactlessly, I told her I couldn't even imagine that kind of thinking and privately thought she must have made it up.

My Jewish peers, especially other children of survivor families, widely shared these views. We lacked any identification with Germany, although my father noted in a 1951 letter that his sons spoke some German with an English accent. I have no such memory, but I think I was told later that we were attacked in school because of the accent and my parents vowed never to speak German in front of us again.

I understand why I developed that attitude and am not proud of it. Ironically, when I dealt with Germans face-to-face, I was usually exquisitely polite because my mother had impressed that value on me. In working with German students at the universities where I taught, I bent over backward to act respectfully toward them, but my heart was not in it. For example, when I learned that most of the fatalities from the 2000 Concorde plane crash in Paris were German tourists on their way home, I told my wife it was a good start. Being a better person than me, she grimaced.

Given these attitudes, it was not hard to imagine my grandparents and father as despised outsiders in their small town. The German census of 1925 enumerated just how geographically isolated they were.

Residents of Großröhrsdorf by Religion in 1925

Group	Number
Lutheran	7,889
Others	382
Catholic	89
Reform	8
Jews	4

The four Jews, the Schönwalds, accounted for just 0.048 percent of the town's population.[2] Most Jews in Germany lived on islands surrounded by a sea of Christians, but the Schönwalds, who were even more geographically isolated, inhabited a mere speck of rock in a vast ocean teeming with crosses. To connect with Jewish life, they had to rely on the institutions built by the 5,000 or so Jewish residents in Dresden. My father became a bar mitzvah in the synagogue there because Großröhrsdorf had no Jewish community. The Dresden synagogue, designed by the famous architect Gottfried Semper and built in 1838, was destroyed by fire per Nazi orders a century later during Kristallnacht.

The family did not convert to Christianity as did some Jews who sought to avoid certain restrictions even before the Nazis came to power. They listed their son as "Mosaich" on his birth certificate in 1912 and reported their Jewishness on numerous other government documents. Even so, my father was not raised in a religious family.

In a fictitious interview published on the 50th anniversary of Kristallnacht in a regional newspaper, local historians Norbert Littig, Matthias Mieth, and Eckhard Hennig had my grandfather acknowledge that he was not a practicing Jew even though he had been exposed to Judaism by celebrating holidays and learning the stories of the patriarchs in childhood. He summarized his religious perspective as "Never forget to show kindness and to share what you have with others, for such are the sacrifices which God approves" – language from the New Testament (Hebrews 13:16) rather than the Hebrew Bible.

---

2. Figures taken from: "Großröhrsdorf," *Historisches Ortsverzeichnis von Sachsen* [Historical Gazetteer of Saxony], https://hov.isgv.de/R%C3%B6hrsdorf,_Gro%C3%9F-_(2).

Although the interview was not real, the characterization corresponds with the facts. With a minimal background, my father arrived in the United States with little understanding of Judaism and no facility at all in Hebrew. When my grandfather advised my father to seek out a Jewish man in New York who had "great connections" that might help them obtain visas, my grandfather described the man as very religious. He warned my father, "Don't mention the fact that you don't believe in it," and further told his son not to call the man on Saturdays. In all the letters to my father, there were frequent references to birthdays and anniversaries but no mention of any Jewish holiday.

Even if the Schönwald family was not religious, their entire social network was decidedly Jewish. All the courses they took to prepare for America were organized by the Jewish community of Berlin. My parents reproduced that kind of tribal society in the United States and were both very active in Jewish communal life.

Oddly to me, my parents still had some pride in being German. They did not disguise their anger about their treatment at the hands of Nazis. My father had reason to despise Germany more fulsomely than I did and sometimes showed it. In 1962, the year I turned 13, he drove my brother and me to Omaha to see the movie "Judgment at Nuremberg" about the war crimes trials of Nazi leaders by the Allies. I remember him explaining to me over dinner before the screening what "sterilization" meant. In the movie, the character played movingly by Judy Garland, a woman with a mental deficiency, testified about being sterilized as a young girl. I'm sure my parents had discussed carefully what we needed to know to understand the movie, and forced sterilization was part of the lessons.

Some years later when I was considering what summer courses to take at college, I mentioned to my father that I was thinking about taking one on German language. My father remarked, not entirely whimsically, that he was considering breaking my arm. Both parents had gone to great lengths when we were growing up to prevent us from learning German, not just because it was the secret language they spoke to one another when trying to keep things from us. Ironically, they spoke two different dialects of German. My father wrote to a friend that my mother could neither speak nor understand his Saxon German due to her upbringing near Heidelberg and was impatient with her accent. "If I had a [German] mark for every syllable she swallows," he informed his correspondent in 1951, "I'd be a very rich man."[3]

Although our family was acculturated to American life, we were not without some tribal sentiments. In particular, we joined most Jews in boycotting Germany. The American-Jewish community promoted a boycott of German goods shortly after Hitler assumed power in 1933, hoping to pressure Germany to end its anti-Jewish activities. Many American Jews continued to punish Germany for its sins against our people long after World War II. As I recall my childhood, those Jews who broke ranks, say, by buying a Mercedes or other German-made goods, earned communal disapproval, possibly mixed with a bit of envy. The Wald household toed the line.

Near the end of his life, after my brother and I had left home and established our own careers, my father shocked us by purchasing an Audi. He wanted German technology, although we had boycotted German products for years. I confess that I later bought a Volkswagen Rabbit, a transgression punished by karmic forces because it was one of the worst cars I ever owned.

Yet my father did occasionally express pride about some aspects of his German heritage. He admired its low-cost public transportation and national health insurance, business-friendly policies he thought the United States should adopt despite his Republican partisanship. When the National Gallery of Art in Washington showed an exhibit on "The Splendor of Dresden" in 1978, my father flew to Washington to see it. He even met with the German curator and discovered they had some connections. The soundtrack in our house was usually operatic, another German influence, and my mother cooked German cuisine rather than the Eastern European dishes that are considered traditional Jewish food.

My mother was fond of saying that you had only to scratch a German to discover an antisemite. Yet she developed a close friendship with a German-born woman in her retirement community and liked filling her apartment with German-made glass and pottery. She compared the United States unfavorably to Germany in terms of coffee and artistic taste, teaching us to avoid weak coffee and kitschy paintings. Like my father, she was a deep patriot because the United States had saved her life.

Because my father never returned to his hometown for a visit, I assumed

---

3. Letter from Henry Wald to Rudolf Nitzsche, January 1986.

that he despised Großröhrsdorf and cut off all ties to its population after he reached the United States. As I accumulated documents, I was surprised to learn that he did maintain friendly relations with some people in the town. In April 1939, barely a month after his arrival on American soil, his mother rebuked him for writing first to a school friend and his family's former maid and only then to his sister.

After World War II when he had witnessed the full extent of the German genocide and learned of his parents' deaths at the hands of the regime, I expected him to have broken all ties to Germany. So did a Jewish family friend who had escaped to the United States from Dresden. She wrote him in 1945, "During all those years that we didn't hear from you, my thoughts were with you. I thought you were taking part in the invasion, and I imagined you walking through the streets of Großröhrsdorf and taking revenge on the bunch of criminals who made us suffer so much." Yet in 1947, he wrote to Hedwig Brodauf, who had been a nanny (*Kindermädchen*) to my father and aunt. He asked for her recipe for crumb cake (*Streusselkuchen*), which was promptly provided. *Frau* Brodauf provided a list of ingredients for a dish that probably contributed to my father's late-life type 2 diabetes. They included copious amounts of butter, sugar, eggs, chocolate, sweet almonds, vanilla sugar, and pudding powder.

I was staggered at first by Hedwig's plaintive requests to her former charge, whom she greeted so fondly as "My dear Heini":

> "I remember the years when you were a little boy, oh beloved Heini, I wish we could see each other again. ... I think you and Suse should come here together, of course only you can decide. ... Beloved Heinz, would you all like to come to Germany again? Naturally not in such a Germany as was in 1933 until now. I hope that I will still be alive the day that you both return to the house that your parents built for you."

I wondered how she could imagine him wanting to set foot in Germany again, let alone live there, but realized from other comments in the letter that she still saw him as the child she had loved in a household with parents she had admired. She even asked for photos of his American home so she could share them with her family. That my father kept her letter tells me that he still had a tender spot in his heart for the woman who had helped raise him and for the family's longtime housekeeper, Martha.

In 1951, my father replied in German to "my dear Gerhard," a resident of Großröhrsdorf, who had initiated the correspondence with his "dear former school and childhood friend Heinz." My father reported that he was very excited to receive the letter and wanted to learn about his former high school classmates. Of the 168 students who had been enrolled, Gerhard informed him, fully a fourth were either dead or still missing from the war. He told Herr Riessenegger, the correspondent, that he hoped some of his surviving school friends would write to him in the United States and bring him up to date. He even apologized profusely for his inability to return to Germany to attend a planned school reunion. He also asked his correspondent to forgive his poor German that had grown rusty, although one of my translators, a native German speaker, said he wrote with perfect spelling and grammar.

My grandparents had considered themselves German to the core. My grandfather had won a World War I military decoration, an Iron Cross 2nd class, and my grandmother's sister Johanna, who lived with my grandparents in Berlin, was made a war widow by that same conflict. The Iron Cross was not displayed on civilian clothing but was signified by a ribbon worn on the jacket pocket. According to an expert on German military decorations, my grandfather's photos invariably showed him adorned with a *Kämpferband*, a black-and-white "fighter's ribbon" indicating he was at or near the front.[4] He was 34 when war broke out, and it was unusual for a man that age to be so close to combat. He also received a World War I service medal, a common decoration introduced in 1934 but notable in that it was bestowed on Jewish veterans *after* Hitler had already come to power. That medal was apparently brought to the United States when my father immigrated.

My grandfather probably believed along with the thousands of other Jewish volunteers that their devotion to the Fatherland would bring about full emancipation. When Hitler became chancellor in 1933, the decorated veteran might well have thought that his obvious display of patriotism would insulate him from the Nazis. In that, of course, he was fatally mistaken.

My grandparents had moved to Großröhrsdorf from Berlin probably because their first-born son, Edi (my uncle, strange to say), had died the year before in 1911 during an influenza epidemic. On March 15, they opened a

---

4. Geoffrey Giles, professor of history at the University of Florida, kindly shared his expertise about these military decorations.

modest textile store, perhaps modeled on the business built by my father's Grandmother Agnes in Berlin. They subsequently moved to a larger building and built their dream store in 1928. It was the largest commercial building in Großröhrsdorf and the surrounding region. A postcard featured a photograph of the store, attesting to its prominence.

The adjective "textile" does not do justice to a business that offered a wide range of products such as ready-to-wear clothing and other goods. The German term *Kaufhaus* in the title denotes a department store. The family's household occupied rooms above the ground floor, a common practice in Europe at the time, and leased out other rooms to individuals and businesses.

My grandparents were considered model employers and there was fierce competition for the limited number of staff positions available in their store. They typically employed six or seven shop assistants and a dresser plus the four family members. When I met with descendants of the employees years later, they let me know how much their relatives appreciated their jobs and working conditions.

The family forged an extremely close connection with a non-Jewish woman who did household chores for them. Even after they were forced to move to Berlin, "Schönwalds' Martha," as she was known to all, visited her former employers in 1939 despite the risks of socializing openly with Jews. My grandparents told my father fondly that their small-town maid was so excited about the visit to Berlin that she probably hadn't slept for days. Martha and the aforementioned nanny Hedwig, known variously as Heppa or Hebbor, also joined the Schönwalds in Berlin to celebrate my grandfather's 60th birthday in 1940, underlining how they were considered part of the family. They must have missed the memo about Aryan racial purity.

In 1937, the Kaufhaus Schönwald celebrated 25 years in business by taking out a full-page advertisement in the local newspaper. They also invited friends and customers to a reception. This celebration occurred a full four years after the Nazis launched an economic boycott against German Jews. On April 1, 1933, stormtroopers from the SA (*Sturmabteilung*), a Nazi paramilitary group specializing in intimidation and street violence, massed outside Jewish-owned department stores and retail establishments and the offices of professionals such as doctors and lawyers. As recounted by the US Holocaust Memorial Museum, they painted the Star of David on doors and windows to identify Jewish-owned establishments and posted signs urging German consumers to avoid them. When the demonstrators took violent action against Jews and Jewish property, the police chose not to intervene. The Nazis justified the action, which continued in place for several years, as retribution for what they called anti-German agitation instigated by world Jewry.

The boycott eventually came to Großröhrsdorf. To discourage customers from visiting the Schönwald store, local Nazis set up an observation post in the Café Martini across the street. They photographed anyone who entered the building and posted enlarged pictures of the customers so the public could shun the "race traitors" who continued to patronize the town's only Jewish-owned business.

Despite these efforts, the boycott largely failed. As a local historian later wrote:

> The *Rödertal-Anzeiger* [the local newspaper published by the municipality], which appears three times a week, did not publish an article against the Jewish department store between 1933 and 1936. Schönwalds were able to advertise their product range in the *Anzeiger* like all other institutions. Mass meetings [later] were organized in the large localities in Großröhrsdorf to convince the population of the "dangerousness of the Jewish race." ... Curt Schönwald was denounced with the lie that he had "beaten a German schoolchild." ... On [April 16, 1938] appeared ... the clear demand: "Germans in town and country, do not buy from the Jew!"[5]

The efforts to incite the citizens against the town's only Jewish family bore some fruit on April 14, 1938, Maundy (Holy) Thursday, when a group of overexcited Nazis attacked and vandalized the store through the night and into Good Friday. Six months before the Kristallnacht pogrom, the crowd seemed to have rehearsed by destroying the store's many display windows.

Although the boycott might have deterred some shoppers, many women in the town worked as seamstresses and depended on the store to provide them with supplies. When economic times were challenging, as they often were in Weimar Germany, my grandparents allowed purchases on credit, something no other store would do. The women whose relatives had

---

5. Thomas Drendel, "At Großröhrsdorf civil courage showed," *Sächsiche De*, November 8. 2018.

worked in the store told me that this generosity often meant the difference between eating and starving, particularly for families with unemployed husbands during the lean years of the '20s and '30s. Norbert unearthed the logbook of one seamstress covering from 1935 to 1945. Even during the height of the boycott, she purchased 90 percent of her supplies from the store.

To avoid detection, some of the women sent their children into the store through a side entrance that was hidden from the Nazi observation-post cameras. Once inside, the large cabinets lining the aisles blocked the line of sight. The children paid for the supplies and then passed them to their parents when safely out of camera range.

The efforts to bankrupt the store appear to have failed. Two shop assistants later recalled that even the top local Nazis only complied outwardly, effectively subverting the boycott by permitting their wives to buy their modish fashions at Kaufhaus Schönwald. Rather than losing business as the boycott continued, the shop added staff through 1938.

Even though the store survived, my father later reported, the Nazi boycott and harassment made my grandfather's life miserable. I suspect my grandfather also was demoralized by Nazis who denied his very identity as a patriotic German who served the nation during World War I. Once a respected merchant, decorated war veteran, and generous benefactor, he became merely "the Jew Schönwald" in their eyes. No indignity was too small to inflict. His listing in the Berlin phonebook made clear he was a disrespected "other" by substituting "Israel" for his given middle name and printing a bold Star of David next to his entry. No other religious group was so honored.

The Schönwalds' integration in Großröhrsdorf before Kristallnacht was also apparent in their relationship with the local "Black, Red, Gold Banner of the Reich." Affiliated with the German Social Democrats, this guild resembled a militia. My grandparents sponsored the organization and advertised in its yearbook. Heinz Dobrint, a member of the organization, recalled in a 2001 interview that my grandparents provided members' free green uniform shirts, which distinguished them from the Nazi militias known informally as the browns (SA) and blacks (SS).[6] When threats against the store began in 1933, members of the group kept watch on the building, surrounding it with guards to discourage attacks by their right-

---

6. Transcript, interview of Hans Dobrint by Norbert Littig, Kamenz, March 13, 2004.

wing opponents.[7] However, by 1938, the year of the Kristallnacht pogrom, the group had been forcibly disbanded and its leader fled to avoid arrest and imprisonment.

My grandparents had a reputation as civic-minded philanthropists. In his 2001 interview, Dobrint said, "Mr. Schönwald has done a lot for poor people." They are said to have donated significantly to building the new public baths, the Massenei-Bad Großröhrsdorf, reputedly the best in all Saxony. When the Nazis came to power, the baths posted a sign refusing entry to Jews and dogs. My grandparents could not step into the facilities that their generosity and community spirit helped build. One photo shows my father as a young adult cavorting at the pool with friends, the Nazi flag visible on the diving tower. This picture was probably taken in 1936 when Germany briefly relaxed its discriminatory laws for the Berlin Olympics. As late as 1985, when he first wrote to my father, Reinhard Gebler assured him that "the name Schönwald is still well remembered and is only spoken with praise and respect."[8]

None of the respect and affection my grandparents earned through their hard work and generosity mattered when Kristallnacht struck on November 10, 1938. From 2:30 to 4:30 a.m., a crowd of Nazi party members supervised the methodical destruction of all the shop windows and entryways. I was told that the Nazis who trashed the store forced the parish sexton to toll the church bells to recruit more rioters, an account that corresponds to the mayor's diary.

The vandals also painted a Star of David on an exterior wall. Repeatedly after the war, efforts were made to paint over it yet the star always reappeared when the paint dried. As a local observer commented: "It is as though the star would not allow the night of terror and violence to be forgotten, and therefore would never allow itself to be successfully hidden."[9] Sometime in the 1960s, the stained plaster was removed and the star finally disappeared.

The town newspaper, which had benefited from more than 25 years of paid advertising by my grandparents, faithfully reported the event from the Nazi

---

7. Drendel, "At Großröhrsdorf."
8. Letter from Reinhard Gebler to Henry Wald, September 30, 1985.
9. *Unser Projekt Stolperstein Großröhrsdorf*, 5. This booklet was privately published by a group of residents interested in identifying and commemorating Jewish homes and businesses in their community. It is based on an unpublished biography of the Schönwald family by Kathleen Schreier. For background on the debate about "stumble stones" in Großröhrsdorf, see "*Sie fordern Stolpersteine zum Gedenken*," *Sächsische De*, June 6, 2008.

perspective. Kristallnacht was, as the paper proclaimed, a spontaneous mass demonstration by German patriots angered by the assassination of a German diplomat at the Paris embassy. The attacker was a young Polish Jew whose parents had been deported:

"After the announcement of the death of [Ernst vom] Rath, who fell victim to a Jewish killer's bullet in Paris in secret treachery, a nightly anti-Jewish plot took place in our village," the paper reported. "The demonstrators gathered in front of the Jewish Department Store Schönwald and smashed the windows of the business building. The excitement of the crowd [was] appeased only when the owner had been taken into protective custody."[10]

Norbert describes the crowd as a small group of "overzealous National Socialist party members" yelling "Jews out!" Drawing on eyewitness testimony, he reports that: "Curt and Regina Schönwald appeared in the door wearing their bathrobes, and spoke the words: 'Gentlemen, what can we do for you?' They were forcibly removed from the threshold and were made to watch as rocks were thrown through the store windows. Curt Schönwald yelled: 'What do you want from me?! I fought in the war and have the Iron Cross 2nd Class.'"

They were driven to the local jail and put in a holding cell overnight. My grandmother was released from custody the next day, but my grandfather, like thousands of Jewish men across Germany, was sent by train to detention in the Buchenwald concentration camp.

The Nazis worked hard to encourage a festive atmosphere as if the town had been liberated from Jewish control. Norbert provides the details:

> The next day, on November 10, 1938, school director Neumann came to the *Hauptschule* [secondary school] and reported to the class: "Last night we chased out the Jew Schönwald. While being arrested he supposedly still said: "My dears, what can I do for you?" Some witnesses said that the teacher took the class to the department store in order to show the children "what the just hatred of the people can do." The saleswomen arriving that morning were shocked. Mayor

---

10. Norbert Littig, *Erbaut 1928 CS: Erinnerung an die Jüdische Familie Schönwald aus Großröhrsdorf* [Built in 1928 C.S. Remembrance of the Jewish Schönwald Family from Großröhrsdorf] (Großröhrsdorf, Germany, 2008), self-published, chapter 7. He quotes from an article, "Örtliches und Sächsisches [Locals and Saxons]" *Anzeiger,* November 11, 1938. Unless otherwise noted, Littig's book is the source for subsequent descriptions of Kristallnacht in Großröhrsdorf.

Rosig came and arrogantly sat in one of the department store's chairs. The saleswomen had to remove the goods from the shattered windows and clean the glass off the textiles. One of them remembers still years later how an SA man, on the day after Kristallnacht, told her: "You should prefer to clean up crap rather than help a Jew."

Some backlash arose when townspeople in Großröhrsdorf saw the respected family driven through the streets to the local jail. As Johannes Gebler noted in his journal – which required more than a little courage to write given the dangers of saying anything negative about Nazism – the residents "condemned this approach in the strongest terms."[11] Decrying the sympathy for my grandparents shown by some townspeople, the Nazi speaker at a celebratory meeting a week later declared it "unfortunate" that the Nazis had to encounter Aryan townspeople who pitied the treatment of these "poor Jews."[12]

The brief detention in the city jail was just a prologue to the torment visited on my grandfather in November 1938. The three weeks he was held at Buchenwald may not sound like much of an ordeal, but the horrific conditions in the camp left him with both physical and, I suspect, even deeper psychological damage. In requiring him to sell his business to an Aryan if he wanted to be released, the Nazis stripped him of his identity as a respected, civic-minded businessman, philanthropist, and decorated veteran of World War I.

Buchenwald existed as a prison camp before the sudden incarceration of almost 10,000 Jewish men in early November.[13] The camp had nowhere to house the new prisoners as the trains carrying them rolled in. The new arrivals, cold, tired, and disoriented, sat outside watching other prisoners throw together flimsy barracks that were neither sealed against rain nor insulated from the November cold. When they finally entered their new "home," they found no floors to prevent rainwater from congealing the ground into mud and a mere two latrines, which were open trenches. In many cases, they had no beds. During the daytime, they were often forced to stand at attention for hours at a time and must have slept fitfully, if at all,

---

11. Quoted in Littig, *Erbaut 1928 CS*, 230.
12. Drendel, "At Großröhrsdorf," 2018.
13. This account of Buchenwald is drawn from Kim Wünschmann, *Before Auschwitz: Jewish Prisoners in the Prewar Concentration Camps* (Cambridge, MA: Harvard University Press, 2015).

as they awaited beatings from random SS raids. I hope my grandfather found a way to numb his feelings on his release. Although he didn't realize it at the time, there would be even worse to come.

Being the kind of man he was, he said nothing in the letters to my father about Buchenwald, but I imagine he relived the mistreatment and humiliation every day of his remaining life. To add insult to injury, the Nazis routinely shaved the heads of those who were released to stigmatize them as prisoners and convicts. Although humiliating Jews was for the Nazis a happy byproduct of the so-called "action," its central purpose was to increase pressure on Jews to emigrate, enabling the state to steal their property. In my grandfather's case, the state won. On his return to Großröhrsdorf, he took steps to "sell" his property to an Aryan, a merchant from a nearby town named Carl Seifert whom my grandfather described in a letter as "that louse." The purchase price of 92,000 Reichsmarks was equivalent to about $37,000.

Whatever the number, it was a fiction, a sham. The Nazis demanded that my grandfather pay off the remaining mortgage on the building rather than allow the new owner to assume the loan. The mortgage was higher than the purchase price, meaning it consumed all of the proceeds from the sale. Simply put, the store was stolen. When the store reopened under Seifert on December 1, 1938, just three weeks after Kristallnacht, the new owner did not need even to cover the iconic "CS, built 1928" that Curt Schönwald had proudly displayed above the main store entrance for the last ten years. Despite the ghostly Star of David on the outside wall, the store could now advertise itself as Arisch [Aryan] in Nazi-approved language.

Deprived of livelihood and home, the Schönwalds moved to an apartment in the Schöneberg neighborhood of Berlin. A few months later, my grandmother informed my father that their dispossession was complete – a new tenant had taken over their old apartment at the store. They took out a three-year lease on their new domicile in Berlin. They were allowed to live in the building because it was owned by an Aryan, but all the occupants were Jewish and the local Jewish Council petitioned the government to turn over any apartments left by Jews who were "evacuated" (i.e., deported) to other Jews in need of housing. It was a "Jews House" in Nazi parlance.

Much to my surprise, I discovered that the portrait of my grandparents I'd seen in childhood was taken in 1939 after they had left for Berlin. Instead of the wary and disoriented expressions I might have expected so soon after the disruption of their lives, the photo sent a different message. Even without a home, business, or future, after countless humiliations, they were resolute. In truth, if I hadn't known how much they delighted in the company of children, I would have been a bit intimidated by the two tenacious grandparents I never had a chance to meet. I think of them as proud but never prideful.

East Germany, established after World War II in what had been the Russian zone of occupation, never properly compensated the family for the Third Reich's theft of its property. After the war in 1946, my father was informed in a letter that the new mayor put pressure on Seifert so that "Herr Schönwald can reclaim his business and house at any time."[14] The process would involve regaining the upstairs apartments, once the family's home, which several tenants and a dental practice occupied. No method to return property had yet been implemented and the writer promised to work on resolving the issue. My father was later told that the building had been nationalized.

My father could not afford to buy the building back in 1946 when he was struggling with full-time study and a full-time job in the United States, and he would certainly have rejected the idea of paying a thief for stealing from him. Furthermore, he had no interest in returning to Germany. After the reunification of Germany in 1990, the nationalized building was eventually returned to private ownership and once again became commercial space. It took some time, but the family did eventually receive some compensation from the democratic government.

I don't know how my father felt about his experiences in the town. Despite being the only Jewish boy, he had school friends. When he graduated from high school in 1928, his yearbook was festooned with poems and comments from fellow students of both sexes who inscribed their friendship on its pages. I've already mentioned photographs of him as a young adult hanging out with friends at the public baths. After fleeing to the United States, he never went back to Großröhrsdorf for a visit, but that could have been due to the difficulty of traveling to East Germany and concern that the communists might detain him for having emigrated. When his school planned a reunion in early 1986, he told organizers that he might attend if arrangements were suitable and talked about possibly taking along his oldest grandchild to see Germany. My father died that February, so the trip did not happen.

Even though he softened his attitude to Germany somewhat and was cordial in his postwar letters to a few town residents whom he remembered

---

14. Letter from Waldemier Bauer to Henry Wald, September 19, 1946.

fondly, my father remained at best ambivalent about Großröhrsdorf. In a 1979 letter to his sister in South Africa, he wrote:

> "Did I really say in one of my previous letters that 'Großröhrsdorf had been good to us'? Please let me know and I'll take your word for it. That phrase does not sound like something I would actually write, but I may be wrong and if I did, it was certainly a bad choice of words."[15]

To me, the most telling sign of his attitude was his longtime refusal to seek compensation from Germany for the death of his parents, something he dismissed as "blood money." He and my mother fought about this refusal because she wanted to bleed Germany dry through any means possible. He eventually cosigned the application for property compensation because Suse said she needed the money and Germany would only grant claims if all family survivors signed on. Eventually, he received the princely sum of $1,373.12 from the German government via the Guaranty Trust Company in New York. I can easily envision my father donating the money to a Jewish cause. I honestly don't know if he would have been pleased by my decision to visit the town years later.

Having visited my father's hometown, learned about my grandparents from their letters, and paid my respects to them at their last home in Germany, I thought my journey was over. I could not know that the odyssey had just begun, that even though I finally knew about the past, the harder part – the journey to reconciliation – still lay in the future.

As for my parents, there was a different aspect to the story. They had their own struggles to survive the Nazis, find a way out of the country, establish a path into a different country, and make new lives for themselves.

---

15. Letter from Henry Wald to Alfred and Suse Lachmanns, September 29, 1979.

PART 2
THE SURVIVORS

5 ORDEALS

Several friends have told me that I pursue my family's history because I want to understand my father. One of my favorite writers once said that the critic explains to an author what the author means to say. My friends/critics have persuaded me that this motivation is indeed at least partly what drives me. As part of that drive, I will try to explain the experiences that molded my father.

Like most Holocaust survivors, my father did not talk much to us about his life in Germany. We picked up snippets in conversation and occasionally overheard him discussing his past with other people. When we asked questions, he told us we would have to wait for him to write his memoirs, something he'd promised to do in retirement. The pledge was not redeemed because of his fatal heart attack during his last scheduled week of work.

My father's reluctance to share his personal history, and his tendency to disclose only occasional fragments, left gaping holes in our knowledge. We eventually grasped that he had been traumatized by what happened to him after the Nazis came to power in 1933, but we lacked specifics. The six years between Hitler's appointment as chancellor and my father's departure from Germany were blank. We were also unclear how he managed to get out of Germany and legally enter the United States.

I've filled in some of these gaps from his papers and the reminiscences of friends and relatives but even more so from his public testimony during a 1978 Holocaust remembrance event in Lincoln. It was held at our synagogue in April, just ahead of the scheduled NBC broadcast of a galvanizing television series on the Holocaust. He was one of four survivors to recount their experiences. I'd been long gone from Lincoln by then and don't remember hearing anything about it. One of the panelists, Eli Modenstein, a video editor at a local television station, later provided me with a tape. Eli, who spent three years in Auschwitz, was the last remaining member of the close-knit network of Holocaust survivors who settled in Lincoln. He lived to 103 before dying in 2021.

When Hitler began his public agitation with the failed Munich coup in 1923, Jews took little notice, according to my father. They did not read *Mein Kampf*, the book wherein Hitler laid out his vision of a Jew-free Germany. Even when Hitler gained office as chancellor in 1933, my father said, the Jewish community did not see it as a serious threat. Some of the disbelief came from identity: "We were Germans," my father said almost matter-of-factly, referring to the family's 300 years in the country. He had established that number based on a family tree he compiled in high school. My grandfather's voluntary enlistment in World War I, when he served as administrative officer of an Air Force fighter squadron, also seemed credential enough to ward off any attacks.

Living as respected citizens in a small town may also have blinded my grandparents to what was coming. "They were friends of ours," my father said of their many acquaintances years later. "What were they going to do to us?" He would then almost bellow the answer to his own question: "Nothing!"

My grandparents were probably reassured by friends who told them that once Hitler had gotten rid of the communists, the elites would get rid of him. Indeed, the historian Marion Kaplan, a participant on the Fulbright German study tour I took in 2000, argued that such reassurances provided by well-meaning friends and neighbors likely dissuaded many nervous German Jews from attempting to emigrate when there was still time to get out.[1] They believed there was no reason to panic.

As the atmosphere for Jews got worse over time and my father was falsely arrested on charges of violating the Nuremberg laws in 1937, he decided it was time to leave Germany. The first step was to obtain an affidavit of support from a permanent resident of the United States. The sponsorship, a guarantee that the newcomer would not become what was called a "public charge" upon the United States, was essential for admission under US

---

1. Marion Kaplan, *Between Dignity and Despair: Jewish Life in Nazi Germany* (New York: Oxford University Press, 1998).

immigration law (then and now) and carried the most weight if it came from a relative already established and gainfully employed in America.

My father must have contacted his American cousin, Hans Peter Gossman, sometime in the spring of 1938, months before Kristallnacht but not long after the mini-riot against the family store during Easter. Gossman first wrote on his behalf to the American consul in Berlin on June 10 of that year.[2] His formal affidavit is dated September 28, 1938, five weeks before Kristallnacht. Gossman was a physician in Rochester, New York, who had arrived as an immigrant from Berlin in the summer of 1934 and was just submitting his own citizenship papers when he heard from my father.

Dr. Gossman described my father as his cousin, and there are occasional references to people with the Gossman surname in the letters my grandparents wrote to their son.[3] My grandfather told my father that he was supporting Gossman's two elderly aunts who remained in Germany, a claim confirmed by the report about his finances when he was facing deportation. Gossman's affidavit assured American immigration officials that the applicant would be an asset to his new country. Having known him since early childhood, Gossman assured the American consul in Berlin that my father was "a very sincere, intelligent, capable and ambitious boy." Gossman was 11 years older than his cousin and had not seen him for at least four years when my father was just 22, so his reference to him as a boy was not unreasonable. On arrival in the United States, my father was met by Hans and lived with the family for a time in Mount Vernon, a Westchester County suburb, before departing for what he thought would be better opportunities in Manhattan.

I had never heard of Dr. Gossman until I found the affidavit. I eventually contacted one of his daughters who did not know about her father's sponsorship or have any materials about it. She told me that he went into the US Army as a physician during World War II, serving as a medic with combat troops, and wrote to his wife about the trauma of seeing the survivors in several liberated death camps.

Ironically, he was one of the Army physicians who attended to the surviving inmates in Buchenwald, where my grandfather had been imprisoned. According to the Mount Vernon newspaper, Gossman used his role as chief medical officer to insist that bodies of Jewish victims found in

---

2. Letter from Hugo Gossman to American Consulate, Berlin, June 10, 1938.
3. Letter from Hugo Gossman to American Consulate, Berlin, September 15, 1938.

the camp be buried in individual graves with headstones in German.[4] He told a reporter that he insisted on it so the Germans under his command could not escape their responsibility for the slaughter. To underscore that point, he required the German hospital staff to place fresh flowers on the graves every day. I have not encountered any communication between him and my father, although there were hints of tension among the cousins in some letters.

Before my father could leave Germany, Kristallnacht occurred.[5] In his 1978 talk, my father recalled what happened in a manner that would be comical if not for the deadly serious nature of this watershed event in German-Jewish history. My grandfather and father were arrested by the town's chief of police and taken into what was euphemistically called "protective custody" at the local jail. The police chief was a friend of my grandfather's and they had served together in World War I. To compound the irony, the chief's son was a close friend of my father and had been dating his sister, Suse. I can imagine how awkward the son must have felt. I was not surprised when my father reported that the police chief kept apologizing for the arrest during the hours they spent in lockup. He told them sorrowfully that he had to do it.

Around midnight, my father said, my grandfather and he were handcuffed and loaded into a truck that took them to Dresden. They were put on a train bound for Buchenwald near Weimar, a 24-hour trip. At his 1978 public testimony, my father solemnly told the audience: "Forty years later, I still remember that train ride." My father, who had little patience for pop psychology or therapy, actually said out loud that the experience traumatized him and mentioned still having nightmares about it.

The passengers were forced to kneel, chained in the position to a bench running the length of the fourth-class railcar. They maintained the position for the entire ride. For a young man of 26 like himself, he said, it wasn't too much of a physical ordeal, but it was much harder on the older men, some in their seventies and eighties.

They arrived at Buchenwald, which was a prison, not yet an extermination camp. Even so, as one historian emphasized, it was purposely built as a "city of terror."[6] It had been meant to house 10,000 to 12,000 inmates, but after

---

4. "Captain Gossman Tells of Work in Atrocity Areas," *Daily Argus* (Mount Vernon, NY), July 9, 1945.
5. For more information on this event, consult Martin Gilbert, *Kristallnacht: Prelude to Destruction* (New York: HarperCollins, 2006).
6. Wünschmann, *Before Auschwitz*, 133.

four days of receiving trainloads of Kristallnacht victims from across Germany, it held an estimated 30,000 Jewish detainees. Apart from Jews, my father said he remembered seeing a fair number of Roman Catholics, some in clerical garb, as well as many communists who were detained illegally. The crush of inmates meant they were not fed after the trip and were soon put into hard labor. They had little to eat, minimal sleep, and almost no protection from the November weather.

In his public presentation my father recalled carrying 100-pound cement sacks and breaking up large rocks with sledgehammers, tasks he called "make-work" designed more to torment prisoners than serve any useful purpose. He may have exaggerated because I'm not sure a young man weighing only about 145 pounds could carry a 100-pound sack of cement.[7] What made the setting particularly horrible, he said, was the absence of information about the length of their imprisonment. It destroyed hope for numerous inmates and drove many to suicide. The camp was guarded by soldiers with submachine guns and surrounded by an electrified fence 10 to 12 feet high. The setting made suicide a simple task of running toward the guards to be shot or into the fence to be electrocuted. He said he witnessed enough self-inflicted deaths for a lifetime.

According to the Tracing Service of the International Red Cross Committee in Switzerland, my grandfather was released on November 27, about three weeks after being arrested.[8] No reason was given beyond the generic term "action," which can mean many things.

Bribery secured the release, my father said. They had arrived at the camp with about $300, the day's receipts from the store, which they had planned to deposit in the bank. Because of Kristallnacht, they were arrested before they could get there. By monitoring camp scuttlebutt, they found a guard amenable to bribery and gave him the cash. Thanks to "honor among thieves," as my father put it, the man came through. He did not sneak them out of camp but must have pushed them to the head of the exit line.

I am much less clear about what happened next. In a letter written more than 40 years later to a resident of Großröhrsdorf, my father said he left Germany for good in 1938. He told the Lincoln audience in 1978 that he crossed the border into Czechoslovakia, only about 80 kilometers [50 miles]

---

7. When he registered for the World War II draft in Lincoln, Henry listed his weight. He registered only a couple of years after the Buchenwald confinement.
8. Letter from G. Wilke, International Tracing Service to Kenneth D. Wald, September 22, 2000.

from Großröhrsdorf, and then made his way via France to Switzerland where he remained until he could get all the necessary papers to leave permanently for the United States.

As difficult as it was to get out of Germany and into the United States, the immediate challenge was securing money for transportation and living expenses. The German government confiscated most of the departing Jews' funds, which made the task even more difficult. Since at least 1934, my father had been stockpiling cash, some in Germany, some with his uncle, Lothar Schönwald, in Switzerland, anticipating he might need to leave Germany on short notice.

He had managed to scrape together about $1,000 (equivalent to about $20,000 today) which he apparently smuggled out of Germany when he left.[9] As he later admitted to his sister, "discovery of this money would have been fatal for me," but he had no alternative. To show American immigration authorities that he had resources, he also asked Uncle Lothar to send a letter of credit of $1,000 in his name to a New York bank, which was duly transmitted. Although he told the Gestapo officers monitoring Jewish emigrants' departure that the money awaiting in New York was sent by Lothar as a gift, the funds had previously been given to his uncle for safekeeping. Had the Nazis realized that the money came from my father's personal funds, which the Nazis routinely stole, it would have meant a death sentence.

The financial transactions with his uncle strained their relationship. As the letters he received from his parents were replete with complaints of Lothar's bad faith in both romantic and financial relationships, my father should not have been surprised that monetary entanglements with his uncle would end badly. Even Lothar's son Gerard later told me he thought his father was in the wrong.[10]

My father never forgot how he had to beg and scrounge for the funds to escape Germany. When Lothar's only son wanted to move from Switzerland to the United States after the war, my father provided him

---

9. My father told my brother that he actually exchanged the money for gold and had it melted down and painted to look like small rocks that he carried in his pocket when he arrived in New York. We looked for these objects in his safe deposit box after Henry's death but found nothing that resembles that description. I am dubious about the claim.

10. Letter from Gerard W. Schoenwald to Kenneth D. Wald and Robin West, September 3, 1987. My father wrote a long letter to his sister, describing in great detail his dealings with his uncle after Lothar must have spoken to an attorney in Lincoln. The attorney, who had worked with my father, apparently refused the case and passed the information along to my father. Letter from Henry Wald to Suse and Alfred Lachmann, December 5, 1985.

with an affidavit of support and some useful advice about dealing with American immigration authorities.[11] I'm happy to report that Gerard and I connected many years later when he was living in California. My father also managed to pay it forward by providing affidavits to his sister and brother-in-law when they were considering relocating from South Africa to the United States.

He eventually reached London to board a German ship bound for New York on March 15, 1939 – just two weeks after his parents had left Großröhrsdorf for Berlin. My mother told me that he had a bad experience in England when a relative on his mother's side treated him as a poor relation – perhaps not inaccurately given the circumstances. Despite my efforts during multiple stays in the United Kingdom, I've never located this person. My father seemed to have a penchant for feuding with relatives, which accentuated the feeling that we had virtually nobody outside of our immediate family.

Heinz became Henry when he arrived in New York on March 20, 1939, aboard the S.S. Europa, the same ship that had shortly before carried to New York the infamous Nazi film director and Hitler pet Leni Riefenstahl.

The passenger list contained a special section for aliens arriving from foreign ports. On the manifest, individuals were listed by last name and then first name.[12] The original entry, "Schönwald, Heinz Israel," was edited by hand to replace "Israel" with his given middle name, Werner. Restoring his actual middle name might have been a simple administrative correction, but I suspect it was done at my father's insistence and was meant to sever his association with anything done by the Nazis. While he later changed his first and last names to become Henry Wald, he never dropped Werner. The form listed him as a merchant who could read both English and German and, following the strange immigration classification of the time, declared his race as Hebrew though he spoke not a word of the language. The passenger manifest indicated that his immigration visa was issued on February 14, 1939, in Berlin and that his last permanent residence was also Berlin, not Großröhrsdorf. That error will become important in considering his experience during Kristallnacht.

About a month later, despite having arrived with a medical certificate noting his defective vision, he was issued an identification card by the US Immigration and Naturalization Service. He was thus entitled to

---

11. Letter from Henry Wald to Gerard Schoenwald, July 25, 1948.
12. "List or Manifest of Alien Passengers for the United States," S.S. Europa, March 15, 1939.

permanent residence in the United States but would have to wait several years for citizenship. Initially, he had a hard time in New York finding a job suiting his talents. But the presence of family no doubt eased the transition, for in a letter dated April 5, just two weeks after his arrival, his mother told him, "I'm very happy that you have the Gossmanns and that they are all so nice to you."

That would end the story of his time in Germany but for one complication: The documents do not support his account of his arrest and imprisonment in Buchenwald in 1938.

The International Tracing Service of the Red Cross has a record of my grandfather's imprisonment in Buchenwald but nothing about my father's. His sister, who left Germany several months after him, flatly told me in 1996 that my father was not arrested on Kristallnacht but was in Berlin, which is consistent with my father's claim in his biosketch to have worked there from August 1937 through January 1939. As an employee rather than a business owner, he would not have been arrested in Berlin. A judicious man, Norbert is certain that my father was never in Buchenwald.

Documents can be misplaced or destroyed, are prone to error, and are unreliable, leaving me with an easy way to sustain my belief that my father told the truth in his televised testimony. When I replay the video of his 1978 appearance, I find it difficult to believe that he was not describing what he experienced. My father was not much of an actor and did not look or sound like somebody who was masquerading as something or somebody he was not. In the written questionnaire he had to fill out in 1942 for the Selective Service System, he indicated his willingness to serve in the US military as an opportunity to exact revenge on Germany for his confinement in a concentration camp for the high crime of being Jewish.[13]

However, according to evidence uncovered by Norbert, he may well have been a prisoner elsewhere at another time. In his profile of my father, Norbert writes that my father "was imprisoned in 1937 for alleged 'racial defilement'" as reported by the local newspaper on May 24.[14] Defilement referred to any romantic or sexual relations between an Aryan and non-Aryan. The local newspaper coverage of the arrest was peculiar because it referred to the accused as merely the "Jewish branch manager of a local

---

13. Henry W. Wald, "Alien's Personal History Statement," submitted to Lancaster County (Nebraska) Selective Service Board #1, June 17, 1942. I am grateful to the US National Archives in Kansas City, Missouri, for providing this document.
14. Norbert Littig, *Erbaut 1928 C S*, 63.

clothing factory."[15] Given the extreme antisemitism of the time, it's hard to understand why the newspaper report did not choose to inflame public sentiment by giving the names of the business (which was not a factory) or the alleged perpetrator. Doing so might have given a boost to the ongoing attempt to encourage a public boycott of the Kaufhaus. Perhaps those pieces of information did not need to be supplied because they were common knowledge or, given the way the Nazis acted based on rumor, there was no foundation for them.

Norbert believes that the charge was made up simply to attack the town's only Jewish family. The *Anzeiger* published another scurrilous article about a year later, alleging bizarrely that my grandfather had struck a German schoolboy and lied about it.[16] My father might simply have been flirting or been seen having coffee with one of the salesclerks at the store, reason enough perhaps for somebody to denounce him to the authorities. In many cases, the informers who reported such liaisons were family members who felt they needed to protect their Aryan women from Jewish men. No indictment was ever filed.

I have no way of knowing with certainty how long he was jailed without trial or an indictment or whether he was taken to a concentration camp for violating the racial purity law. It would not have been beyond the Nazis' warped legal practices to send him away for three weeks of hard labor based on mere suspicion of race mixing. Fortunately, I do not have to rely entirely on supposition because some circumstantial evidence suggests that my father was indeed incarcerated for having social relations with a German (that is, Aryan) woman or women before Kristallnacht.

Located just 64 kilometers [40 miles] from Dresden, the Sachsenburg concentration camp housed a separate company of Jewish inmates who had been classified as race defilers.[17] Among other tasks, these prisoners were assigned to break up rocks in quarries along the adjoining Zschopau River. The memoirs of some inmates describe this work as completely useless, meant more to exhaust and degrade than any other purpose. At Buchenwald, by contrast, the Jewish "November prisoners" jailed during Kristallnacht were not assigned to work details but were kept apart from the general population of inmates. The concentration of prisoners accused of race mixing [his alleged offense], the camp's proximity to Großröhrsdorf, and the make-work assignment that my father remembered in his 1978

---

15. Norbert Littig, *Erbaut 1928 C S*, 63_65.
16. "Örtliches," *Anzeiger*, April 16, 1938, note from Norbert Littig, November 6, 2007.
17. Wünschmann, *Before Auschwitz*, 146.

public talk are consistent with his imprisonment in Sachsenburg for a few weeks in 1937. If that happened – and the evidence falls short of definitive confirmation – it's possible he blended his own experiences at Sachsenburg with his father's later ordeal in Buchenwald.

This puzzling incident adds support to my aunt's claim that he was in Berlin and thus was not arrested in Großröhrsdorf during Kristallnacht.

Nonetheless, the arrest prompted him to leave Großröhrsdorf for the relative safety and anonymity of Berlin sometime in the summer of 1937. One of the saleswomen at the store recalled helping him pack boxes for his sudden move to the capital.[18] Norbert is certain that my father was in Berlin from 1937 until he departed from Germany in late 1938.

It has taken me some time to come to terms with the possibility that my father was not an inmate at Buchenwald with his father, that he was not manacled to a seat on his knees during the long train ride. Knowing how he blamed himself for failing to get his parents out of Germany and how that perceived failure ate away at him, I can understand that he may have needed to put himself mentally on that train with his father and the other men arrested on Kristallnacht. In some way, I think he felt he deserved to have been punished for what he – and he alone – considered his betrayal of his parents' needs. I do not think he was trying to gain any advantage and never even heard him describe himself as a survivor. Yet, where his parents were concerned, he showed all the signs of severe survivor guilt.

Most Holocaust survivors were not in concentration or labor camps but were, like him, fleeing persecution from the Nazis or their puppets in other countries.[19] He was driven to believe he had been imprisoned, I surmise, because he needed to think of himself as a person who warranted punishment even if his parents recognized how much he had labored and sacrificed to obtain their freedom. The idea was already implanted when he filled out his alien registration form in June 1942. I don't doubt that he believed he had been in a camp, a scenario not uncommon in studies of memory. The story was true to him, I think, but I do not completely discount the possibility that he told a genuinely true story.

---

18. Norbert Littig, *Erbaut 1928 C S*, 63–65.
19. Robert Rozett and Shmuel Spector, *Encyclopedia of the Holocaust* (New York: Routledge. 2013), 427–28.

6 BECOMING A YANKEE

As little as I knew about how my father survived in Germany, I knew even less about his early years in the United States. Some of his experiences as a new immigrant were revealed in his parents' letters as they tried to buck up his spirits. But I was mostly ignorant about his transition to American life, the move to Lincoln, and his military service. His self-imposed code of silence, broken rarely, frustrated my efforts to understand him better as a man and father.

My father was a complicated man. In social situations, he was charming, articulate, and outgoing. He had learned some English from his mother and studied it in school. On arriving in 1939, he listed himself as fluent in both English and German. However, as he told a German friend many years later, he discovered that the English he learned in school was the British version and could not be easily understood by many of his new countrymen.[1] He came by the accent naturally because his mother, although born in Berlin, spent 15 years of her childhood in England, obtaining her education and then working in her father's business until she returned to Germany in 1905. After just two years in the United States, she complimented him on writing "in a wonderful American-English style" and speculated that he probably spoke like a native-born American, too.[2]

I suspect she considered British English as the gold standard, perhaps

---

1. Letter from Henry Wald to Reinhard Gebler, December 4, 1985.
2. Letter from Curt and Regina Schönwald to Henry Wald, May 26, 1941.

explaining why she complained about the "bad" accents of fellow students in her conversational English class in Berlin. Success in America, my father said, required him to learn to speak "like a Yankee." He told my brother and me that he schooled himself to speak American English by attending movies. He watched the same films over and over until he could understand and pronounce every word in the American manner.

Most people who met him assumed he was a native English speaker. You had to listen carefully to detect even a hint of German. His "yeah" sounded like the German *"ja"* (as does mine) but wasn't very noticeable. During the Nixon years, my father made fun of Henry Kissinger's heavy German accent. My father noted with pride that he could speak English with barely a trace of an accent despite arriving in the United States at an older age. He suspected that Kissinger cultivated the Prussian accent purposely to give himself a worldly air.

My father had an explosive temper that he usually manifested by shouting and occasionally throwing things. Over the years, my father and his sister had several exchanges about the origin of bad tempers in our family. My aunt once told me there was no such tendency among the Schönwalds, so it must have been imported from my mother's Rothschild clan, which would conveniently exonerate my father. However, he alluded to bad tempers among their grandmother's family, the Proskauers, in a 1985 letter to his sister – Proskauer was his grandmother's maiden name and Uncle Adolph was their uncle and, eventually, Suse's father-in-law: "The Proskauers were a very temperamental clan, amen. And as far as I remember, Uncle Adolph could also be said to have a temper at times."[3]

Whoever bequeathed these behavioral tendencies, my father certainly received a large dose. The ire emerged most often when my father was stressed and tired, a common condition for an accountant during income tax season before the age of computers. Being awakened from an afternoon nap by the telephone sent him into a rage, prompting my brother and me to pounce on the phone the moment it rang as if we were football players instinctively covering a fumble. Small annoyances could also prompt him to lash out. My wife, raised in a more easygoing household, was astonished when she first heard him erupt, and his little grandson was devastated the first time his beloved grandfather yelled at him.

Despite his temper, he was a good father and husband who did not use physical and emotional violence. As little children, my brother and I sat in

---

3. Letter from Henry Wald to Suse Lachmann, December 5, 1985.

his lap to recite evening prayers and exchanged a kiss and hugs as we went off to bed. We knew we were loved, and we also knew how hard he worked to support the family. He was engaged in our lives, becoming the president of the local youth baseball league even though he did not understand the basic rules of the game and usually cheered at the wrong times. If he had ever tried to coach or umpire, I doubt baseball would have survived. When we traveled to a major league town, he got us tickets to games and even arranged for us to attend the 1960 All-Star Game in Kansas City, Missouri. Like many refugees in the United States, he believed that playing baseball somehow turned an immigrant into a real American.

There was some tension in our home, of course, but we were not a dysfunctional family. Most of the friction arose because my parents were trying to raise German kids in an American environment. They did not want us to be German but rather to exhibit what they felt were the traits of a good child in the German mode – obedience, orderliness, respect for adults, neatness, studiousness, good grooming, and so on. Some of our friends, most of whom were third- or fourth-generation Americans, modeled very different behavioral styles. These patterns are common to the immigrant story.[4] My brother and I were good kids, but our parents still hassled us about things that we thought were trivial like hair length and our use of "um" when speaking. I recall my father once getting mad when "The Ed Sullivan Show" featured Sly and the Family Stone, practitioners of a music style that he did not admire. Who gets mad about that?

I asked my mother after he died why he had such a temper. She believed that he blamed himself for the death of his parents, for not getting them out of Germany in time. He thought he could have saved them if only he had worked harder. From my grandparents' letters and some documents in his files, I know that he moved heaven and earth to get them out. At great personal sacrifice, he accumulated the money to purchase their passage and mailed the tickets to them. He could not forgive himself and seethed inwardly until frustration produced an eruption.

He began to talk more freely about his experiences as he got older, especially in the 1978 appearance, but he told those stories after my brother and I had left town. While attending Sabbath services at our Lincoln

---

4. Years ago, I read an account by a young Cuban-American woman who arrived in the United States during the Mariel boatlift. She had achieved great success despite her modest circumstances and was admitted to an elite university. She said her friends had a name for immigrant kids who did not study, behave well, or think carefully about their actions: "Americans."

synagogue shortly after I arrived for his funeral in 1986, a friend of his pulled me aside and recounted an anecdote my father had told him about his military service in World War II. I also learned more when I viewed the tape of the 1978 appearance.

Back in 2000, when I first visited Großröhrsdorf, I asked the residents what they remembered about my father. Most instead volunteered their recollections of my grandparents and several told me they had been at school with his sister. I had pictures that showed him as an adolescent and a young man with friends, but nobody talked about that. As I worked on essays about the letters, I felt guilty about paying so much attention to my grandparents at my father's expense.

Unlike the other fathers in our largely working-class neighborhood, mine was not given to mechanical undertakings. If he knew anything about car engines, he kept that knowledge well hidden. When he decided to take up photography, he filled his workroom with equipment for developing film and produced many prints that invariably cut off the heads of his subjects. He had a workbench strewn with tools he seldom used and rarely to good effect.

Even changing a light bulb was a challenge because he believed that bulbs should be screwed in so tightly that it was almost impossible to remove them without breaking them. I think he worried they might flee if not permanently attached to the fixture. When I was planning to come home for Thanksgiving during graduate school, my mother asked me to arrive around lunchtime, long before my father came home from work. I thought there was a problem she wanted to discuss and brooded a bit about it as I drove back to Lincoln. When I arrived, she greeted me with a box of light bulbs and a list of burned-out ones. Her goal was to get me home early enough to prevent my father from replacing them, which generally included hiring an electrician to fix the damage.

Beyond keeping quiet about his experiences under the Hitler regime, my father also kept silent about his military service. He offered only a few passing references to basic training. Even if I had wanted to research it on my own, I would have learned little because his military records were destroyed by a 1973 fire at the National Personnel Records Center in St. Louis. After his death, I did find a few military records in his files, and a trip to the US National Archives in Maryland enabled me to reconstruct a good portion.

As a native German, my father was classified as an enemy alien upon arriving. The government did not intern him and he had begun to make a life for himself when the war broke out. Unlike the loyalty of many US-born German Americans who sympathized with Hitler, that of the German Jews who escaped Nazi Germany could be assumed by the government. Like other German-born immigrants of draft age (he was 28), he registered in 1940, a year and a half after arriving in New York. Responding to a questionnaire that he completed on June 17, 1942, my father made clear where he stood, saying, "To prove that I am definitely an enemy of the Nazis I will only have to state that I am Jewish. I for one have a personal score to settle with the Nazis which includes revenge for three weeks in a concentration camp where I was taken only because I am Jewish."[5]

Those answers were sufficient to get him drafted within the year, just a month after his marriage when he was working in Casper, Wyoming, for a metal salvage plant owned by Northwestern Metals in Lincoln. After induction at Fort Warren near Cheyenne on October 15, 1942, he was sent to Fort Sill in Lawton, Oklahoma, for basic training and stayed for advanced training in field artillery.[6] I recall him making fun of his military record at Fort Sill. He claimed he was demoted due to the actions of other GIs in his unit. One of them, a country boy, tried to impress a girlfriend from the area by loading a big piece of artillery on a trailer and hauling it off base to the young woman's home on a Sunday. The GI's effort must have worked because he didn't have time to return it to base. When the unit convened for training on Monday, they couldn't find the huge gun. My father was blamed for the disappearance and demoted.

Because my father was rather sedentary and not physically gifted, I assumed he had an uneventful wartime and I could not understand why he claimed his activity was classified and could not be discussed in public. That assumption was undercut the more I learned.

While still training in artillery, he was plucked out of Oklahoma and sent to one of the Army's specialized training programs at Stanford University. The program was intended "to ensure a continuous flow of technically and professionally trained men for the prosecution of the war" by sending enlisted men to universities for specialized studies that would enhance the

---

5. Attachment to "Alien's Personal History Statement," submitted to Lancaster County (NE) Selective Service Board #1, June 17, 1942.
6. Statement by H. P. Manning, Army Specialized Training Program, Re: Order 587, 1943. An addendum to his final pay voucher states his induction site as Fort Logan, Colorado.

war effort.[7] I had already found his Stanford transcript and library card in his files, so this information filled in one of the blanks about his record. He and his classmates, mostly German-born Jewish refugees, took courses in history, foreign languages, and policing.[8]

My brother and I were raised to believe that getting a grade less than an A was a moral failing: Had we been Catholic, it would have been considered a mortal sin. When I proudly displayed a college grade report with all A's, my father asked why I hadn't received an A+. Told that they didn't issue such grades, he insisted that I would have received them if I had worked harder. So it came as a great surprise and disappointment to discover that he earned only one A, one B, and three grades of "pass" at Stanford. The three passes were from pass-fail courses, but, I would argue, he would have gotten an A+ if he had tried harder.

I once heard my father tell somebody about his German class at Stanford. His classmates, native German speakers, were required to take the course in their mother tongue. As was the case in the Army, he said, the instructor was a native English speaker who had learned his German in American schools. Because they knew more than the instructor, the students covered for one another if someone chose to skip class, saying "present" when the instructor would call out the person's name on the roster. One day, when one of the truant Army enrollees didn't respond to his name, the instructor repeated it and waited for an answer. "What's the matter?" he asked after a minute of silence, "Doesn't Ginsburg have any friends?"

I had assumed that my father spent the war years translating German documents at a desk somewhere in the United States. That would be nothing dishonorable, but it wasn't exactly combat at close quarters. However, his discharge papers indicated that he was a member of Company E of the 2nd Military Intelligence Training Battalion. My father? Suddenly, I had an inkling that his assignment went beyond a desk job.

If they did not put much effort into German class, the students sent to Stanford did take their intelligence training seriously. The colonel and chief of the Military Intelligence Service (MIS) in San Francisco so informed his

---

7. See "The Army Specialized Training Program and the Army Ground Forces," reprinted from *The Army Ground Forces, The Procurement and Training of Ground Combat Troops*, by Robert R. Palmer, Bell I. Wiley, and William R. Keast (Historical Section, Army Ground Forces Historical Division, Dept. of the Army, Washington, DC, 1948), 28–39.
8. Most of the other 17 students in his Army Specialized Training Program cohort mentioned in a letter by their commander had names that suggested German or other European Jewish ancestries. Some, like my father, may have changed their names to sound less foreign.

counterpart in Washington.⁹ The foreign-born trainees showed "considerable enthusiasm" by giving up leaves and evenings to get their reports accurate to the last detail. In fact, he reported, "A number of them skipped their last night of liberty before entraining in order to have information in our hands the last day," and others continued to work on them as they rode the rails. To underline their dedication, he encouraged his fellow officer to "appreciate what this must have meant to an enlisted man." Henry W. Wald, the name he took legally in April 1943 when he received citizenship after completing basic training, was one of the 17 men praised in the memo. He kept the memo and a personal letter of thanks from the chief of military intelligence.[10]

What were these reports? I assume they mostly compiled "order of battle" documents relating to the disposition of German military assets and local Nazi leadership in the parts of Germany where they had lived. It is unclear whether the reports referred to by the MIS chief involved on-site research or not.

I learned of the next step in his military career by serendipity in 2005 when I received a note from a man named Bernie Lubran.[11] He told me that his late father, Walter, and mine had served together at Camp Ritchie, Maryland, during World War II. When my father was discharged from the Army, Walter asked him to write a letter to explain to his mother what her son was doing at Camp Ritchie. My father complied and wrote a long letter to Mrs. Lubran in Pittsburgh.[12] Bernie discovered the letter among his mother's belongings after her passing, tracked me down, and sent me the letter. He assumed I knew what he meant when he described our fathers as "Ritchie Boys."

The Ritchie Boys were American soldiers recruited to a newly formed military intelligence unit, the first of its kind in the US military. Suddenly, the pieces of the puzzle came together. They were native speakers of German who were trained to collect information in Europe. Virtually all of them were German Jews. Most of them followed the US troops into Germany after D-Day and stayed until the European war was won.

By another coincidence, a German filmmaker had just produced a

---

9. Letter from Col. Warren J. Clear, Military Intelligence Service (San Francisco) to Lt. Gen. John G. Groome Jr., Military Intelligence Service (Washington, DC), September 20, 1933.
10. Letter from Col. Warren J. Clear, Military Intelligence Service (San Francisco) to PFC Henry Wald, September 24, 1943.
11. Email from Bernie Lubran to Kenneth D. Wald, January 4, 2005.
12. Letter from Henry W. Wald to Mrs. Lubran, February 12, 1944.

documentary about the unit. *The Ritchie Boys* featured interviews with veterans from the unit about their exploits in Europe. Though almost every one of them insisted that "they were no soldiers," they displayed astonishing creativity in wheedling information out of captured German troops. Some of the reports sent home by their commanders praised their ability to ferret out information that saved the lives of many American GIs. Bruce Henderson's 2017 book, *Scholars and Soldiers*, recounts their exploits in more detail. While I was a visiting professor at the University of Michigan in the fall semester of 2011, I went to an exhibit about the unit at the Detroit Holocaust Memorial Center. I was escorted by the curator, Guy Stern, a retired professor from Wayne State University who featured prominently in the documentary.

Although the Ritchie Boys displayed bravery and imagination, some of the field reports about them were not entirely complimentary and confirmed their modesty about their military prowess.[13] One report to the Military Intelligence Training Command observed that many of them "were unfitted [sic] for training for life in the field, particularly under battle conditions." Their commanders deplored that these soldiers "cannot drive army vehicles" and "know nothing about first echelon maintenance." It was a fair criticism – many of the German Jews came from densely populated urban areas where public transportation far outstripped private automobile ownership. In their defense, the street smarts to survive New York might have prepared them for battle conditions.

The United States was fighting a war against antisemites, but some officers seemed less than sympathetic to the cause when they evaluated the Ritchie Boys. One colonel from the 12th Army Group complained churlishly about "some central European with a thick guttural accent and no other qualification than the accident of birth in a German-speaking country ... [who] struts around with a Prussian air of superiority, wearing Master Sergeant stripes."[14] He was particularly exercised that these usurpers were given ranks that should have gone by rights to "men of background, breeding and education." Lacking a deep understanding of the language and culture of the enemy country, however, such men would have been as useless as, I suspect, the colonel himself.

---

13. The records of the Ritchie Boys are generally found at the National Archives facility in College Park, Maryland, under Record Group 165.4, Records of the Military Intelligence Division (MID, G-2), 1900–50. The comments about the military skills of the G-2 are from a report by Gen Edwin L. Silbert, "Ritchie Graduates in France: Composite Reports from G-2," November 29, 1944.
14. Assessment dated December 8, 1944.

PFC Wald arrived at Camp Ritchie in May 1943. A letter to the Military Intelligence Service in Washington had mentioned the sudden and surprising departure of the class of trainees from California to Maryland, and my father's letter to Bernie Lubran's mother indicated that his stationing there obviously had been a mistake. The unexpected transfer of the Stanford cohort was part of a reduction in Army Specialized Training Program enrollment intended to free up more personnel for combat in the upcoming invasion of Europe. Perhaps by referring to a mistake, my father meant to indicate that his impaired vision made him unfit for combat. While most of the program's students were sent to infantry units, those from the Stanford group continued in military intelligence at Camp Ritchie. Germany had wanted to kill them, but their knowledge of the country and the language saved them and allowed them to exact revenge on the country that had brutalized them.

Although he was duly noted in the official record as a trainee at Camp Ritchie, my father's name does not appear on any of the grade rosters from his time there and is absent from any other files I examined. What did he do during the roughly six months between his arrival and departure?[15] The only thing I know for sure is that he and Walter Lubran occasionally went on leave in a nearby town and learned more about Camp Ritchie from the locals than they had been told in camp!

The Camp Ritchie files indicate that PFC Wald was discharged from the Army due to poor vision in October 1943. Yet in an undated biosketch I found among his papers, my father reported that he served with the Army as a translator in Europe from August 1943 to August 1945. The biosketch was probably prepared quickly in response to a media request for an event honoring him for service to the Jewish Welfare Federation in Lincoln. The newspaper story about the banquet noted that he served with the British 8th Army in Sicily in 1943 and then with the US 3rd Army under the command of Gen. George C. Patton for the duration of his service. He claimed to have guided the general through a liberated concentration camp and to have watched German civilians being forced to walk through the camps to see the Holocaust with their own eyes. In 1983, writing to an acquaintance in Großröhrsdorf, he reported that he served four-and-a-half years in the

---

15. For daily life in Camp Ritchie, see chapter 3 of Alfred G. Meyer's self-published autobiography, "My Life as a Fish," available at http://www.ritchieboys.com/DL/fish2o3.pdf. Meyer was eight years younger than Henry when he arrived at Ritchie and thus was more typical of the trainees.

military, predominantly in Europe. In October 1945, he returned to his prior place of employment in Wyoming.

There are various holes in the story. How could somebody who had sufficiently good vision to be drafted in 1942 become ineligible to serve in 1943? There are several possibilities. Perhaps, because he was past the age of 30, the Army determined that he was not a strong candidate for an assignment that required rigorous physical work. My father alluded to that possibility when he told Bernie's mother that the training at Camp Ritchie was "stiff," a "game for very young fellows." As for her son, who was the same age as my father, he advised her that Walter "should not attempt to compete there." Another hypothesis is that perhaps the Army purposely misled people about the status of interrogators and intelligence operatives by tampering with their service records. My father could have been in Europe under cover when the Army claimed he was back home. However, the letter to Mrs. Lubran was dated February 12, 1944, written from Casper, Wyoming, and bore a February 14 postmark. Confirming that he was in the United States at that time, he wrote Mrs. Lubran "I am no longer a soldier."

The biggest question is how he could have served with the US Army for two more years after it had discharged him in 1943. When I put this question to various Ritchie Boys I met later, none had an answer. I thought he might have been a civilian employee of another intelligence unit, most likely the Office of Strategic Services (OSS), but the declassified list of OSS personnel at the National Archives does not contain his name. Perhaps he was assigned to the Army's Counterintelligence Corps, whose members wore Army uniforms but no insignia of rank. Kissinger served in that unit after the war ended in Germany.[16] There was no roster of group members in the National Archives.

When I first assembled his timeline, I considered the possibility that my father had made his military career sound much more heroic than it was. After training for military intelligence duties, leaving the Army due to bad eyes sounds anticlimactic, so perhaps he exaggerated his service overseas. I was pretty close to accepting that conclusion when I returned home for my father's funeral.

That's when I first heard the story my father told one of his American friends about his interrogation of somebody from Großröhrsdorf. The German prisoner was astonished that this American GI, wearing an Army

---

16. Niall Ferguson, *Kissinger*. Vol 1. (New York: Penguin, 2015), 158–68.

captain's uniform, spoke perfect German and knew so much about the town. The soldier looked carefully at his interrogator until finally saying, "I know you, you're the Schönwald boy." They had been schoolmates.

I appreciated hearing the story but was skeptical because it sounded too good. I was still inclined to believe that my father had embellished his military history when Norbert wrote to me in 2009.[17] He had recently interviewed an elderly resident of Großröhrsdorf, Rudolf Grossman, who was a World War II veteran of the German army. Aware of Norbert's interest in my family, the man had called to share a story about the Schönwalds. It was the same story that my father had told his friend in Lincoln. Rudolf Grossman was interrogated in Friedberg, Austria, by my father on May 18, 1945.

As Grossman remembered it: "The interrogation officer asked if he was from the Großröhrsdorf near Dresden, which he answered in the affirmative, and if he knew the department store Schönwald. This Grossman also affirmed and enthusiastically told the interrogator that Herr Schönwald always offered and sold his mother very inexpensive clothing for her seven children."

The interrogator convinced the camp doctor that Grossman posed no threat and should be released. The interview had been so cordial that Grossman's friend, who had accompanied him, took a picture of the two natives of Großröhrsdorf. The film was lost when a guard inspected the released prisoner and his friend on their way out of camp, discovered both the camera and a pistol on the friend, and commandeered both items.

Grossman later requested a copy of his discharge certificate. Norbert forwarded it to me.[18] When the envelope with the discharge certificate arrived, I opened it, unfolded it, and spread it on a table. My wife, standing beside me, exclaimed, "That's Henry's writing!"

To further bolster my father's claim about his time in Europe, Norbert located another older man, also from the vicinity of Großröhrsdorf, who remembered being interrogated in a Paris suburb near the end of the war in 1945. The soldier had deserted the German army and, because he spoke English, was arrested under suspicion of being an English agent. The prisoner, Gotthard Senf, recounted how the interrogator, who he presumed was a US Army captain, questioned him in depth about his hometown.

---

17. Interview of Rudolf Grossmann by Norbert Littig, November 11, 2008, Großröhrsdorf.
18. Certificate of Discharge for Rudolf Grossman, May 18, 1945, issued at Ray Barracks, Friedberg, Germany. This document was classified as secret.

"He specifically asked questions about buildings and people in Großröhrsdorf that really only a resident could know," Senf said. When the interrogator elicited the information that Herr Senf's father was named Kurt, he informed the prisoner that "our fathers played cards with each other." The prisoner, whose arrest had been a mistake, recognized his questioner as the son of Curt Schönwald. Senf noted that he was not treated like a prisoner by my father and that his former neighbor bought him food from the officer's cafeteria.[19]

Finally, in an interview in 1996, my mother reminisced about her early married life. She said that my father went to Germany while he was in the Army and described his activities there in a way that sounded like those of the Ritchie Boys. My mother noted that my father told her only that he would be in Europe but not where or when and that he would be safe but would not be able to write her. Together with the other information, this convinces me that my father did serve as an interrogator periodically from 1943–1945.

Dan Gross, a researcher who has concentrated on American Jews in the US military during World War II, offered a plausible hypothesis about my father's service when we communicated in 2013. Dan told me that the Office of War Information (OWI) employed civilians who "were stationed in Europe, given an Army rank (and uniform) and assigned to the Psychological Warfare Division." If one of these civilians spoke German fluently, he might well have conducted interrogations of German soldiers. Dan found no documentation that my father served in OWI – possibly due to the St. Louis fire – but it would explain his presence in uniform as an interrogator.

Failing to mention the Ritchie Boys was not characteristic of a man who talked straight, however. Since the Ritchie Boys did not come to public attention until the 1990s, I think my father believed the information about them was classified, so he held his tongue.

After his military service ended, he returned briefly to Casper and then to Lincoln in mid-1946, where he began to rebuild his life. After just one year of full-time study at the University of Nebraska, he received a bachelor's degree in business administration and passed the state's rigorous certified public accountant (CPA) examination. Both achievements are documented, yet they raise a new mystery.

---

19. Interview of Mr. Gotthard Senf by Norbert Littig, April 3, 2013, Kamenz.

How could my father possibly complete an undergraduate degree in one academic year?[20]

That mystery is easily solved: My father was a returning veteran from a popular war and the university was eager to help ex-soldiers make up for lost time. He was a high school graduate (albeit without records to confirm it), had scored well on Army tests and a standard admissions test, and his English, as I noted, was near native in proficiency. He also presented the university with a notarized letter from Natrona County High School in Casper, certifying that his scores on two other standardized tests entitled him to enjoy "the rights and privileges of a high school graduate."[21] On that basis alone, he was admitted to the university and began his studies in the fall of 1946.

In February 1947, he petitioned the university to waive the requirement for the minimum number of credit hours for the degree.[22] He told the university:

> From 1928 to 1933 I studied at the Institute of Technology at Dresden, Germany; this institution was an accredited university and had several colleges. ... Upon passing the oral examination on March 14, 1932, and on the basis of a thesis on the subject of "Direct and Indirect Taxation: A Comparison and a Program," the academic degree of "Doctor of Economic Sciences"... was conferred upon me. The original of that diploma was likewise lost, but I have secured a duplicate certificate of which a photostatic copy as well as a certified translation are attached.

With that education and his extensive business experience in several enterprises, he surely didn't need all the basic courses normally expected of undergraduates just out of high school. He just wanted the necessary coursework to prepare for the CPA exam.

---

20. According to the transcript, he took just 13 courses at the university for a total of 38 credit hours in two semesters and one summer session. He received an additional 19 hours of credit for the coursework at Stanford and three hours of credit in Military Science in recognition of his military service. That still left him with only about half the 125 credit hours needed for an undergraduate degree in business administration.
21. Letter from S. K. Walsh, Natrona High School, Casper, WY, June 8, 1945.
22. Letter from Henry Wald, February 10, 1947. The letter was addressed "To Whom it May Concern" and did not specifically request a waiver, but it provided justification for that action.

The critical factor that persuaded the university to approve this audacious request was documentation provided by the Technische Universität Dresden.[23] The certificate was issued when my father "asserted under oath that the original copy of his doctor's diploma has been lost." Given the firebombing of Dresden a year earlier, the lack of records is not surprising.

I don't have to speculate about the impact of that German document on the University of Nebraska's decision to waive the normal required minimum coursework and credit hours. His transcript explicitly noted that the degree was granted "on [the] basis of Doctor of Economic Sciences degree – Institute of Technology, Dresden, Germany" as well as the credits earned at Stanford and Nebraska.

The evidence I've accumulated convinces me that he simply had no such graduate degree. The key problem, which Norbert discovered, is timing. After graduating from high school, my father embarked on a vocational-technical track, enabling him to become a businessman, what Germans call a *handler*. He enrolled in several technical colleges until 1931, leaving him no time to have earned a doctorate from the Institute of Technology by early 1932. Moreover, he would not have been admitted there because he had only four years of high school rather than the six years required of applicants.

My father's own statements cast doubt on the claim about the doctorate. He told the 1940 census taker only that he had completed four years of high school. He listed only a grade school and high school degree on the form for the Selective Service System. According to the Camp Ritchie files, he indicated that he attended vocational schools from 1930–1932, which corresponds to the personal documents about this period, but goes on to report that he spent a half year at the Technical Institute of Dresden during 1933.[24] Perhaps more important, my father checked a box for all the other schools he'd mentioned to signify that he had received a diploma but left it unchecked for the Technical Institute. Elsewhere on the form, he described himself as a "salvage man," doing manual labor that involved classifying and sorting different types of metal as well as dismantling autos and engines for scrap. The word "accounting" does not appear on the Army forms.

The Dresden Technical University, as it has been known since 1961, has

---

23. Certificate for Henry Wald from Institute of Technology, Dresden, confirming his receipt of a doctorate, signed by the Rektor (English translation), December 14, 1946.
24. War Department, Military Intelligence Training Center, Camp Ritchie, MD, Form P-21, October 15, 1943.

no record that my father ever attended or graduated from the university and has not been able to locate the dissertation. When Norbert sought more information from the university, the archivist confirmed that the certificate my father presented to the University of Nebraska "looked real" and would only have been issued by the institute in rare cases when the applicant was considered trustworthy.[25] But because of other considerations, the archivist declared that my father had not been a student or graduate of the university.

I wondered if perhaps he defended his doctorate at a later date, by which time universities had begun to expel Jewish students and faculty, but that seems unlikely. My father's biosketch from the 1960s, which says he earned his doctorate in 1933, states he then worked as an accountant in Dresden for four years from April 1933 and then in the same kind of position for the F. W. Woolworth company in Berlin from August 1937 through January 1939. His commercial training was in bookkeeping, but he exaggerated it by likening essentially clerical activity to the analytical tasks required of accountants. In any event, working full time would have allowed him no opportunity to work on a dissertation.

So what did he do from 1933 to 1939? No records confirm that he worked as an accountant in Dresden and Berlin. Rather, It's clear he worked in the family store until he fled Großröhrsdorf after the indictment for race crimes in 1937. His enrollment in the specialized textile program makes sense as preparation for joining the family firm. One of my grandfather's letters notes that my father had worked for him in the family store but doesn't give dates. There are also photographs obtained by Norbert of gatherings of store employees in 1935 and 1936 where my father was present and identified as a junior or assistant manager. In the newspaper account of his 1937 arrest for race mixing, he was also described as the store manager.

Working in the family store would have made sense for another reason. Beginning as early as 1933, Jews were gradually expelled from many employment fields. The bans started with professionals like doctors and lawyers but soon spread to other careers in the public and private sectors alike. My father was thus entering a job market that was increasingly closed to him, so it is likely he joined other German Jews in seeking employment in those Jewish businesses that were not yet Aryanized by the Nazis. Being in a family firm had advantages. I don't know what he did in Berlin after

---

25. Letter, Matthias Lienert, Director of Dresden Technical University, to Norbert Littig, July 29, 2008.

fleeing Großröhrsdorf, but it's plausible that he was employed as a bookkeeper, a job for which he had credentials and experience.

Perhaps his intelligence training had taught him something about subterfuge because he showed some guile in getting the Dresden institute to issue the document. In his waiver letter, he pushed his date of birth back from 1912 to 1908. Befitting a CPA, my father was punctilious about numbers and would never have allowed such an error to pass uncorrected. This incorrect date was sent to the Technical Institute, which duly reported his date of birth as 1908 on the certificate. In the eyes of the rector considering the application, this would give my father an additional four years after completing high school, allowing him to attend graduate school and defend his thesis by 1933 as he claimed. As the Technical Institute was unaware that he had continued his vocational training until the early 1930s, they would not know how little time he would have had to pursue the doctorate and how implausible it was to claim one. I doubt the University of Nebraska looked closely enough at his documentation to notice the four-year age discrepancy between the German certificate and whatever proof of age he claimed on his application.

When he returned to Lincoln in 1946, my father was a decade older than most of the 20-something veterans who were his peers and classmates. The disparity was due to time lost because of emigration and military service. Having a fair amount of practical experience in business management, both in Germany and the United States, he did pick up enough background to hit the ground running. With his wife pregnant with their first child the year he wrote his waiver petition, the pressure was on him to find a way to make a good living quickly. If anyone was to blame, it was my brother, Steve, who timed his gestation so badly that it forced my father to speed up his progress to a degree!

At various times when I was young, my father told me I could do anything I wanted as long as it was a recognized profession, so I imagine that he saw accounting as a good choice for somebody with his bookkeeping training. I don't doubt he took advantage of the postwar crush of returning veterans to reduce the time needed to earn his degree. Given his academic performance at the university (11 A's and 2 B's in an age before grade inflation), the passage of the CPA exam while he was still taking classes, and his stellar professional career, the decision to expedite his studies was a good one even if based on false premises.

I knew how he fiddled his education credentials but am still uncertain why he did it. My hypothesis about his reasons for obtaining the degree fell apart completely when I discovered that Nebraska at the time required a person seeking recognition as a CPA only to (1) hold or be seeking American citizenship; (2) live in or have a place of business in the state; (3) be "over the age of 21 years and of good moral character."[26]

Even if my father did not need the degree to take the CPA exam, the university likely advised him to work toward the degree, the tangible manifestation of his expertise and a useful fallback credential in case he did not pass. He may have decided that a college degree would improve his status and thus the credibility of his firm. Maybe his interaction with other students in accounting generated awareness of the importance of having a degree or stoked his pride and ambitions.

Then again, perhaps Henry saw this as an opportunity to achieve a credential that had been denied to Heinz. As a young man, he showed impressive educational potential. He received two awards for academic achievement from his college preparatory high school in Kamenz and was recognized as an *Obersekundant*, a student of higher caliber. The school of commerce in Cottbus that he attended after high school recognized his "exceptional accomplishment" on the final examination given by the town's Chamber of Industry and Commerce.

A student with that background would probably have continued his education at a college or university. Perhaps, being a dutiful firstborn son, my father acceded to his parents' wishes for a specialized vocational education that would enable him to take over the store eventually. The rising tide of antisemitism in the early 1930s may have persuaded him that a young Jew would not be welcome in a German university. My father was not much of a drinker, and I can't imagine him beating anybody in a sword duel, so perhaps it's best that he skipped the German university experience – he didn't fit in.

Even before receiving his undergraduate business degree, my father began an accounting partnership with a classmate in July 1947 and eventually added a third partner to the growing CPA firm. The firm was successful. However, the erstwhile junior partner engineered the break-up of the firm in 1964, so my parents told me, because he thought they could attract better clients if they didn't have a Jewish partner. Tellingly, my father kept the letter from the disloyal partner in his files.

---

26. William C. Dorsey, *Compiled Statutes of Nebraska 1929* (Lincoln, NE: State Journal Company, 1930), chapter 1, Section 1-101, 63.

This experience caused my parents extreme anguish not just because of the economic security it threatened. The naked prejudice reminded them that they hadn't entirely escaped antisemitism by leaving Germany. My father was particularly wounded by the betrayal of his fellow founding partner, who joined the junior partner in another firm. True to form, neither parent talked much about it to me, but I learned what it meant when my mother suffered an emotional breakdown while the firm was being dissolved. It led to her hospitalization and psychiatric treatment.

I was alone with her at home when she had the episode and could not immediately reach my father or brother by phone. She kept asking me strange questions about whether we were still in Germany and whether my father had business partners, so I knew she was completely disoriented. As a somewhat callow 15-year-old, I was terrified by my mother's emotional collapse and relieved when my father finally came home and called for an ambulance. As she was loaded into the emergency vehicle, my father told the neighbors who had assembled that she had a dizzy spell and would be all right soon. I realized in time that he was embarrassed by mental illness. When we visited her later at the hospital, she was her normal self but asked us what had happened. She may have lost the memory, but I never did.

The firm's break-up turned out to be a blessing in disguise. My father felt he had been carrying the partnership due to the junior partner's tendency to put socializing before business. The firm continued (albeit with a shorter name) with my father as sole partner. He eventually promoted a younger accountant to full partner status and the firm became Wald & Anderson.

My father's clients came from two different worlds. He did taxes and auditing for several businesses owned by fellow Jews in Lincoln but also became connected with companies engaged in ranching, cattle-feeding, and other agricultural enterprises across Nebraska. Since very few Jews were farmers, these clients from the agricultural sector were predominantly Christians. Ironically, considering the junior partner's belief that the firm would do better without a Jewish connection, it was a Jewish businessman in tiny Schuyler, Nebraska, who first connected my father to the ranchers, feedlot operators, and grain elevator owners who significantly augmented the firm's client list. These connections also led in time to several bank directorships that further increased his revenue. I hope my father knew, as I learned from several of his clients at his funeral, that they considered him a friend and virtual family member, somebody they relied upon for advice about life and finances.

The non-Jewish businessmen seemed very exotic to me when they visited him in Lincoln. One earned my lasting gratitude with his annual Christmas gift of a slaughtered cow that provided us with top-quality Nebraska beef throughout the year. We were, I believe, the first family in our neighborhood to have a second freezer. The meat was so ample that my mother gave away any ground beef and decided to cook with only the more refined ground sirloin that we had in abundance.

Yes, there are many holes in the stories from my father, most significantly regarding the truthfulness of his reported experience in a concentration camp. I may appear to be denigrating his memory, portraying my father as a man who played fast and loose with the facts. The untruths about his imprisonment – if that's what they are – do not denigrate his character in my view. The untruths may have been truthful.

My father valued integrity. It showed up in little ways. When we ate out, he always counted out the change he received from the server. If it was too little, he asked for the correct amount back, but he also returned any excess above what he was owed. He exercised the same honesty regarding his business clients.

I remember vividly one day he came home from the office agitated and unnerved. He had learned that one of his best clients (meaning one who generated a lot of revenue for his business) had kept hidden some assets, income that remained unreported on the tax returns my father had filed on this person's behalf. As the tax preparer, he could be held liable for false reporting, but his anger went much deeper than that. He insisted that his clients pay only what they owed, doing battle on their behalf with IRS auditors if need be, but demanded that clients provide him with full and unvarnished information when he prepared their returns. He saw the client's behavior as a betrayal of his code and summarily dropped the client even though it put a significant dent in his earnings.

I understand the mental forces that prompted him to see himself on the train to Buchenwald. They do not diminish him in my eyes nor reduce my respect for the way he rebuilt his life. I respect his military service, believe it to be truthful despite any inconsistencies in the records, and cannot criticize him for doing what he needed to do regarding his education credentials to make a living. His behavior, more than his words, still provides me with a model of integrity.

7 MY MOTHER

My mother, Margarete Mina Rothschild, the daughter of Louis and Celia (known as Cilly), was born in 1913 in Öhringen. I don't know the origin of her first name, but she was given the same (Hebrew) middle name as her paternal grandmother, who had died two years earlier. Known by the German nickname "Gretl" (short for Margarete), she married my father in New York in 1942 and moved with him to Lincoln the same year. She returned to New York to live with her sister and father when he entered the Army in November. After the war, she rejoined him in Casper, Wyoming, for a brief spell until moving back to Lincoln for good in 1946.

My mother experienced the Nazi regime as a young Jewish woman coming of age but did not share her memories of that period until after my father died. Over the next 13 years, her story emerged in small bursts. Lingering at the kitchen table over multiple cups of her industrial-strength coffee, she reminisced about growing up in a small town near Stuttgart and struggling to get herself and her family to the United States.

My memories of some of these conversations are hazy. Fortunately, her stories were preserved, although I didn't realize it then. My mother was never entirely comfortable with English, and her command slipped further after several mini-strokes. I did not understand her when she told me in a phone call that she had made something that week.

"A what?" I asked.

Struggling, she said, "You know... oh, I've forgotten the word. *Um Gottes willen* [For God's sake]!" Assuming she would eventually recall the word, I let it pass and we talked about something else. We never returned to the mysterious "something" she had made or done.

While cleaning out her Lincoln apartment after she died in March 2000, I stumbled on a videotape that turned out to be the "something" she had been trying to tell me about. In 1996, she had been interviewed for Steven Spielberg's Visual History Archive at the University of Southern California.[1]

I was able to make copies of my mother's video to share with the rest of the family. The clerk at the video store mentioned that their machinery routinely displayed the video being copied on monitors around the facility. Normally, she told me, it was just background noise that employees tuned out.. However, this video grabbed their attention. Some had tears in their eyes and looked forward to meeting me when I came.

Öhringen

Like my father, my mother came from a prominent family in her small town.[2] Her father and brother Sam partnered in trading in agricultural products, primarily grains but also horses and cattle. They had a warehouse that stored grain, flour, chocolate, and confectionery as well as stables for livestock. Many Jews in Öhringen – and throughout Germany – were also involved in these agricultural enterprises.

While the Schönwalds had no other Jews in their town, my mother's family had a small Jewish community of about 200 people, and they played an active role in it. Her father was a leader of the synagogue and her mother was president of the Jewish Women's Society.

While my paternal grandfather considered himself a German with Jewish heritage, largely disconnected from religious life, my mother attended religious school twice a week. One of her teachers might have been Joachim Prinz, who was rabbi in Öhringen for a time, immigrated to the United States in 1937, and spoke at the March on Washington in 1963 where Martin Luther King gave his "I Have a Dream" speech. My mother's

---

1. Gretl M. Wald, "Interview 11068," Visual Holocaust Archive Online, University of Southern California, January 19, 1996.
2. Norbert Littig, "The Life of the Jewish Family Rothschild in Öhringen in the Context of their Time," 2011, unpublished.

secular education was not neglected. Like my father 300 miles away in Großröhrsdorf, she finished high school, then attended business school where she learned typing, bookkeeping, and other vocational skills that prepared her to work in her father's business.

The Rothschild family was a part of the town's fabric. Both brothers had served in the army during the First World War and my maternal grandfather belonged to a veterans' association and the local sports club. He had been quite an athlete and was popular in town. The same was apparently true for my mother. A beautiful young woman with jet-black hair, she had an active social life and told me of several young men who pursued her.

My mother recalled a normal childhood in the small town of about 5,000. Life was good, she insisted, and, echoing my father's comment on his 1978 tape, said, "Everybody knew us." The family was affluent, owning a large house and employing a full-time maid like "Schönwalds' Martha," who worked for the family for 25 years and was considered a member of the family. My mother also reported having good relationships with non-Jews and considerable interaction with relatives elsewhere. They hosted so many visiting family members that their house was known informally as the "Hotel Rothschild."

Her life changed drastically in 1931, two years before Hitler attained power, when her mother died after surgery for a blood clot in her leg. Her father, 15 years older than his wife, was then in his mid-50s. My mother said he suffered a complete mental breakdown that required her to take over running the household and fill her father's role in his business. At the age of 17, she also had to raise her 11-year-old sister. She spent much of the time after her mother's death shadowing her grief-stricken father as he walked around town, fearful that he would "do something to himself" – her euphemism for suicide.

These circumstances were difficult enough, but her new role as the titular head of the household was even more challenging because it coincided with the rise of Hitler. Many people in town turned against the family after 1933. Neighbors who once greeted her warmly when they passed now ignored her, and erstwhile friends crossed the street to avoid contact. "Children would spit at you," she said. Shutters were closed every night to protect the windows from rocks thrown at the house by other residents.

The situation deteriorated almost from the moment Hitler assumed power. On March 18, 1933, Norbert reported, the SA undertook a violent police action in Öhringen, rounding up communists, Social Democrats, and Jews. The 17 people arrested were "interrogated, beaten, and sometimes severely mistreated." A photograph of the victims in the prison garage, under a crude sign with a Nazi swastika, appeared in numerous newspapers, setting off global protests and prompting three local pastors to condemn the action.

As the protests indicated, not everybody mutely stood by as their Jewish neighbors were harassed. Some residents braved the wrath of National Socialists by trying to protect Jews, none more than the non-Jewish family close by who ran a butcher shop. Their son, my mother's schoolmate, was smitten with her. Having seen pictures of her as a young woman, I could believe it. When Jews were forbidden to enter the shops or could do so only after dark, when they risked being confronted by roving Nazi gangs seeking Jewish blood, the young man smuggled food to her at night. It took courage and decency.

I asked her once when she realized it was time to get out of Germany. She told me a story that I cannot verify, although she believed it without question. One day in 1936, the Nazis summoned the leader of the town's Jewish community to Stuttgart for interrogation. He returned home on the train later that night – in a sealed coffin. Four men, presumably Gestapo agents, guarded it until it was buried. She believed they didn't want anybody to see what the Nazis had done to the deceased man. It must have been the only occasion in the history of the Third Reich when Gestapo agents sat *Shemira* over a Jewish body.[3] The story was so vivid that I tend to give it credence.

As with the Schönwalds in Großröhrsdorf, the campaign to drive out the Jews struck the Rothschild family business in Öhringen. The local Nazi paper announced in November 1936 that Jewish livestock traders were banned from the local cattle market. The ban cut deeply into a major part of the Rothschild business.

During Kristallnacht, a group of about 50 men invaded the small Jewish synagogue and ransacked it. They were stopped from burning it to the ground only because the Aryan homes and businesses surrounding the synagogue would also have caught fire. According to Norbert, several townspeople living adjacent to the synagogue passively resisted the pogrom by refusing to leave their homes. Stymied, the intruders carted off Torah scrolls and prayer books and set them alight in a nearby plaza. Possibly due to the presence of a group of disgusted onlookers, the leader of the local

---

3. The Jewish custom of remaining with a body until it is buried.

Nazis forbade his fellow bigots from attacking the Rothschild business premises across the street. Early the next year, the municipality bought (extorted) the synagogue building from the local Jewish community.

As with my father's hometown, the local newspaper in Öhringen faithfully adhered to the Nazi line. In its alternate universe, the pogrom was reported as a spontaneous uprising by a population angered that "a certain Jewish clique has made itself talked about a lot" – whatever that means.[4] The funeral pyre that devoured furniture, ritual implements, prayer rolls, mourning pillows, carpets, curtains, and other fittings was celebrated as "the end of Jewish grandeur" rather than a wanton act of arson.

After hearing about a mob forming to kill the Jews, my mother said, her Uncle Sam and two other Jewish men from town fled to nearby Stuttgart to avoid arrest. Samuel rode a bicycle for several kilometers to another town where, unrecognized, he took the train to the city and found refuge with his wife's widowed sister. A year later, Samuel and his wife arrived in the United States.

My mother told me her father was taken to jail and held overnight during Kristallnacht. When she and her sister Ruth visited him in jail the next morning, bringing him food and necessities, they were told he could return home with them. She never understood why he was not sent to a concentration camp like the other arrested men, none of whom she recalled ever returning to Öhringen. She said her father may have been saved because he had once been mayor and a leader of the local gymnastics club. Even in the hierarchical and discipline-oriented German police force, it seems, personal ties could outweigh ideology.

The Rothschild brothers had tried to sell their property before Kristallnacht. The responsibility now fell entirely on my maternal grandfather because his brother remained in hiding until he could leave Germany that year. The outcome was depressingly similar to my father's parents' experience leaving Großröhrsdorf.

The town committed to buying the Rothschilds' business and residential buildings, which were appraised at 11,500 Reichsmarks. By the time the agreement was approved by the district office, the value was adjusted down – by three-quarters! – to 2,900 Reichsmarks. The settlement, for which no record of payment was ever recorded, left the family almost destitute. It

---

4. This recalls a German historian's description of Jews in 1879 as "an alien element that has taken too much space in our life." Quoted in Peter Hayes, *Why? Explaining the Holocaust* (New York, NY: W.W. Norton, 2017), 44.

reduced my mother's father to earning a bit of money by cleaning zippers. Apparently, the war had disrupted the production of this invention, creating demand for cleaning services. He could do this work at his temporary home, a hotel room in Stuttgart.

These concerted efforts ultimately made the town Jew-free. Most of the Jewish residents escaped to the United States or Palestine, but 40 died in concentration camps. In 1949, the town agreed to pay the Jewish community 45,000 Reichsmarks and accept responsibility for caring for the sole Jewish institution in Öhringen, the Jewish cemetery where my grandmother and great-grandmother are buried. Standing in front of those graves, the only trace of the family left in the town, was a moving experience. To its credit, Öhringen posted a plaque on the former synagogue building and invited former Jewish residents for a reunion in 1993. A local group has been raising funds to restore the synagogue and commemorate Kristallnacht. For the 2023 observance, the program focused on the Rothschild family.

To America

When the family decided to get out of Germany, my mother took charge. She acquired the affidavit of financial support from a distant cousin of her father in the United States, somebody she didn't know well. She also badgered the US consul in Stuttgart to obtain the essential visas. She told my wife and me a story about that effort that is not entirely consistent with her account on the taped interview and that I cannot verify independently. She said she sent documents and visa applications for her father, sister, and her to the consul's office in Stuttgart but initially received no response. Realizing it was becoming dangerous to stay, she decided to visit the consulate in person. Having learned how to deal with bureaucracy, she marched into the outer office, strode past a befuddled receptionist, and breezed through the open door into the consul's office.

She said she shut and locked the door behind her and told the man sitting behind a large desk that she needed three visas and would not leave without them. He told her – patronizingly, I imagine – that the consulate didn't operate that way and she would have to wait for the visas to arrive by mail at her home. She responded that she would get the visas that day or she would scream, rip her dress, and accuse him of trying to rape her. She got the visas. They had only enough money to pay the fare for one family member to cross the ocean, so she would go ahead and eventually arrange travel for her father and sister.

Having obtained the visa in early April 1939, she boarded the aptly named S.S. *Manhattan* in Hamburg exactly one week later and arrived in New York after a two-week voyage. She carried a passport that was festooned with swastikas and bore a large, red J (for Jude, or Jewish in German) but did not adhere to the Nazi custom of adding "Sarah" to her name. Perhaps she charmed or threatened some official to ignore the law in her case.

On arrival in New York, her priorities were to accumulate enough money for her sister and father's passage, obtain affidavits of financial support for them, and set up a new household in anticipation of their arrival. These tasks were particularly challenging because she spoke little English. She spent the first three weeks in New York living with a married girlfriend from Öhringen and then found a job as a nanny for two small girls in the home of a physician and his wife. The job suited her because the young girls didn't speak much more English than she did. She was also the housekeeper for an elderly woman and her daughter whom she remembered for their kindness to her.

My mother might have felt less alone in the big city had she realized that one of her first cousins was also living in Manhattan. Leonore Glasner (her married name) was the daughter of one of her uncles, Leopold Rothschild. My mother told me she had never met this uncle who had immigrated to the United States in 1884, had a daughter named Constanza, and, she thought, lived in Key West. The family in Germany had lost all contact with him, and I was unaware of his existence until she casually mentioned him to me one morning at breakfast.

Although government documents report different immigration dates, Uncle Leopold had indeed immigrated to New York and shortened his first name to Leo. He married an American-born woman and lived in the city until dying barely four months before my mother landed. By 1940, Leo's American-born daughter was a schoolteacher whose husband, a Holocaust escapee from Czechoslovakia, owned a small art gallery in Manhattan. Besides teaching, she also wrote the lyrics to several popular songs including one with the less-than-innocent-sounding title "My Face Is Dirty with Kisses" and an equally dubious first line "You made an awful wreck of me, I'm glad it's all in fun." She must have had a name in the music business because she owned a personally autographed photo of Jerome Kern, the towering composer of Broadway and Hollywood musicals. Her middle name was Constance, further confirming her identity as Leopold's daughter. Leonore was almost ten years older than my mother. As far as I know, the two women never met.

Shortly after reaching the United States, my mother resumed efforts to bring over her father and Ruth. A distant cousin of her father had provided the affidavit required for immigration. Otto Mannheimer, her patron, was a wealthy apple dealer and distributor from Rochester, New York. Assuming financial responsibility for my mother posed little risk to him because she was a young woman who could support herself. Once she was in New York, she asked him to provide a similar affidavit for her father. By this time, she told the interviewer, her father and sister were in mortal danger of deportation.

Mr. Mannheimer demurred, fearing that he would have to support my grandfather, who was 66 at the time. He paid for her father's and sister's ship tickets but recommended she seek the affidavits from another wealthy Jew in Rochester, a department store owner who was a generous benefactor of the Jewish community. At the urging of three women for whom she worked as a maid, she took the train to Rochester, went to his office, swept past the receptionist in the outer office, and requested the affidavits.

The man in Rochester agreed but told her he would have the documents notarized and mailed to her. Echoing her experience with the American consulate in Stuttgart, she told him she would not leave without the affidavits. The man found a notary public and she returned to New York with documents in hand. She promptly mailed the affidavits and the ship tickets she had bought to her father, who was still living temporarily in a Stuttgart hotel with his daughter. After nearly a year of my mother working to arrange their emigration, her father and Ruth finally arrived in New York on March 4, 1940.

They shared an apartment at 560 West 163rd Street in Washington Heights, the same neighborhood where my father lived upon arriving in the city. My mother told me she had worked as a nanny and domestic in several homes and painted lamps and other chinaware at a ceramics factory. In the 1940 census, she duly described herself as a factory worker. After her sister arrived, she insisted they work together. I found photographs dated 1941 and 1942 of my mother and Ruth at the Tamiment Resort in the Poconos. They were employees, not guests, wearing the uniforms of maids or kitchen workers.

I've made all this activity sound matter-of-fact, but it is important to emphasize that my mother's achievements were remarkable if not astonishing. She was tiny, shorter by several inches than the five feet she claimed on her US naturalization papers. She never entirely mastered English and spoke with a pronounced German accent. As children, my brother and I made fun of her comic mispronunciations of some words and her rolling "R," which was especially pronounced when she spoke about one of our favorite vacation destinations, the Red Rocks of Colorado. She was beloved in our community but also, I think, considered a bit ditsy. It was easy to underestimate her, as I realized later when she shared her life story with me.

I also found it difficult to envision my mother having acted so boldly in the past because, after my father died, she was paralyzed by indecision. If my brother and I did not 100 percent agree about a course of action, and even if we did, she simply couldn't say yes or no. Instead, as she admitted in a letter to her sister-in-law, she dithered.[5] One day, in frustration, I asked her why she couldn't make what seemed to be the simplest of decisions.

She responded how she had been the head of her household since she was 17, responsible for the house and business, and her father and sister, during the long years of the Nazi nightmare. She decided when and how they would leave, where they would go, and how to get the necessary documents. Alone in New York, she raised funds to book passage and arranged housing once her father and sister followed her to the United States. Only when her sister married a German-Jewish refugee (an American GI) and her father went to live with them could she begin to think about a normal life.[6] At that point, she told me bluntly, "I'd made enough decisions for a lifetime" and was determined to find herself a partner who would take over that responsibility.

My mother found the right man at a 1939 New Year's Eve party in New York. My father had brought another date, and my mother was with another man, too. My father asked my mother to dance, and that sparked a relationship. He had already committed to move to Lincoln (more about that later) and left New York just two weeks later in January 1940. She said they corresponded while he was away. He encouraged her to visit Lincoln because, as an enemy alien, he was not free to travel. When he was deemed draft-worthy in 1942 and regained his ability to travel, he returned briefly to New York to woo her. They were engaged after two weeks and married two weeks after that on October 29 at the luxurious Essex House Hotel across the street from Central Park West. Just two weeks later, he left for basic training in Oklahoma and she returned to New York for the duration

---

5. Letter from Gretl Wald to Suse Lachmann, January 31, 1996.
6. Louis died in 1946.

of his service. She received a stipend from the Army Allotment Plan for soldiers' wives.

My mother told me about a small contretemps at the wedding reception. A friend of my father's from Germany wanted to assure the father of the bride that his new son-in-law had a respectable background. He apparently overdid it some by stressing the prestige, wealth, and reputation that the Schönwalds had enjoyed in their region. My maternal grandfather interpreted this well-meaning gesture as a snide suggestion that my mother had married above her station and lashed out at the man, insisting the Rothschilds were every bit as high society as the family of the groom. Showing that both sides of my family had tempers, my maternal grandfather came close to blows with the much younger man until my father's friend apologized.

The newlyweds did not let their wartime separation cool their ardor for each other. Writing to her husband on January 1, 1943, she mentioned that her father's offhand comment about the possibility of mail being delivered despite the New Year's Day holiday sent her racing downstairs to the mailbox. She was delighted to discover an airmail letter that "dearest Henry" had sent her from the wilds of Oklahoma.

Something in his letter must have raised concern about her efforts to introduce a young woman to a young man they both knew in New York. She apologized vociferously for having given him cause to worry and assured him, "Darling, I am not mad at you because of this letter, in fact, it has shown me how much you love me." And to repay the sentiment, she wrote to her soldier in training, "I cannot even begin to tell you how much I love you. Believe me, I could never again live without you."

My father's only surviving letter to his beloved Gretl arrived nine months later when he was still at Fort Ritchie in Maryland.[7] Knowing my father rarely expressed tender emotions, I simply don't recognize the soulful, besotted young man who composed this romantic love song in prose. He wrote that he regretted he could not be with her to show her how much he loved her. Being with her at special moments, when he could see "her lovely eyes shine," was "all the reward any man could possibly ask for." Their separation would end one day and then, he promised: "Oh boy!" He was prescient, I suppose, because they produced two boys.

When he said she had given his life new meaning, I don't think he was

---

7. Letter from Henry Wald to Gretl Wald, September 12, 1943.

being trite. Both his father and mother had mentioned occasionally that he was prone to depression when things did not go well, and when he wrote the letter, he had known for more than a year that his parents had been deported to Poland, which almost certainly meant they were dead. He had lost almost everything he valued, and his world was turned upside down by his emigration and then induction into the US military.

I do not doubt that marrying my mother gave him new life. Their love and affection for each other was always apparent. He meant it when he told her he thanked his lucky stars each day that fate gave her to him.

Complications

Although my parents were married for 44 years, I neither knew nor suspected that considerable odds worked against them getting together. Of course, that can be said for most marriages in which the partners first meet by chance. But for my parents, it was truly a close call, as I learned from my grandparents' letters to him, which I did not read until after my parents had died.

I hadn't much wondered at first why our father never showed my brother and me the letters. Talking about his parents and telling stories about them would probably have been unbelievably painful because of the (unwarranted) responsibility he felt for their murders. He probably thought that we would have considered them – the letters *and* our distant grandparents – ancient history and having nothing to do with our lives. Like most of his peers, he wanted to put the past behind him and bequeath to his children a more positive legacy. I'm sure he also withheld the letters because he did not want us to live in fear.

It never occurred to me that he might have wanted to hide something from his wife.

Some of the letters told of a serious romance in Lincoln that nearly led to marriage but came to an unhappy end early in 1941. My grandmother blamed the relationship's failure on his risking going deeply into debt to secure his parents' freedom. It impressed me how she consoled him by saying their plight, their desperation to escape Germany, was solely to blame for his unhappiness. An insolvent immigrant without immediate prospects was hardly a promising marriage partner. She took a philosophical tack, saying charitably of the young woman, "It is *impossible* for her to care as much for our fate as you may have asked her to do."

Reading this was an "Oh my God" moment because the date of the letter and other details proved that the young woman in question was not my mother. Goldie Seidmann was the daughter of Morris and Hannah Seidmann, two Russian immigrants who didn't speak English when they arrived in the United States, according to the 1910 census. The couple initially lived in New York and eventually became the parents of two girls. By 1917, the Seidmanns had moved to Lincoln where he worked as a tailor at Gold's, a Jewish-owned department store that was the largest retail establishment in Lincoln. As it happened, Gold's was one of the places my mother worked when she first arrived in Lincoln. The 1930 census revealed that the then-22-year-old Goldy (spelled Goldie in official records) lived in Omaha, Nebraska, and worked as a stenographer for an insurance company. She lived with her married sister Lillian, her brother-in-law, and their little boy.

I knew the names of the family members because my father wrote about them to his parents. Although he only moved to Lincoln in January 1940, his parents were aware of his special friendship with Goldie less than three months later. My grandfather was already hopeful that the young lady would be a good life partner for my father, and my grandmother rather devilishly asked her son to "say hello to your friends from me, especially to HER." When they learned just two weeks later that my father was already looking for a job in Omaha where Goldie lived, both parents suggested he should not rush into marriage.

By early May, my grandparents had become sold on the prospect of marriage. My father sent them photographs of the Seidmann home and a portrait of Goldie. My grandfather admired Goldie for choosing to work even though she did not need to, a sentiment that my father often expressed about several professional women whom he later served as an accountant. My grandfather said he loved my grandmother 30 years earlier as much as my father now loved Goldie and pointedly encouraged his son to follow in his father's footsteps.

Showing more restraint, my grandmother urged him to proceed with sensitivity:

"I can only recommend being nice to her and treating her well. Understanding each other and the feeling of being understood can make your life happy together in the same way that you know it from

> your parents at home. I'm convinced that you've made the right choice."

Leaving no doubt, she ended her letter by sending "best wishes and many kisses to you and also Goldy, with tender love, to you both."

Less likely than his wife to express tender sentiments, my grandfather nonetheless asked my father to send his "warmest regards and kisses to the family Seidmann, especially to Goldy." He also declared soon after that he already considered her a member of their family.

Any plans for a quick marriage were derailed by the sudden and unexpected death of Goldie's father, Morris, at age 55 on August 17, 1940. Even so, my father must have remained optimistic about marriage because his mother expressed her satisfaction at his report that the two of them were in "perfect harmony" just two weeks later. However, things do not seem to have gone smoothly after that as my father and Goldie stayed away from each other for some time. In his last letter of 1940, my grandfather told his son that he hoped for "an agreeable solution for your problems with Goldy." The last mention of Goldie in the Schönwald letters was a reference in August 1941 to my father having seen her again in passing.

There were hints in the letters that Goldie chafed somewhat under my father's assertive behavior as a boyfriend. There may also have been truth in my grandmother's supposition that Goldie, born and raised in the United States, simply couldn't empathize with my father's situation. As my grandmother noted in late October 1940, "Goldy knew from the start what she was getting into. Her parents once came to that country the same way, didn't they? In the end, her heart will have to decide, and if she really loves you, then she will get over anything that may appear to stand in your way."

Two months later, his mother opined with some empathy, "Maybe the fact that you will have to care for us is making her apprehensive. I can see how that could be a problem for her." In the same letter, my grandfather congratulated my father for being sensible enough to end the relationship rather than get married at all costs.

The obstacles were formidable and suggested that the relationship was doomed from the outset. Raising money for his parents' passage, obtaining sufficient funds to satisfy US authorities that his parents would not be destitute, and earning enough to satisfy the needs of four people would certainly drive him into debt. He was desperately trying to improve himself by attending university and holding down a second job on top of his position at Northwestern Metals. Admirable though they were, these efforts probably consumed his energy, reinforced his pessimistic nature, and raised doubts in Goldie's mind that he could be a good provider and attentive partner.

Ironically, the very things that caused Goldie and my father to grow apart probably helped persuade my father and mother that they had found the right match. My mother, a fellow penniless immigrant, was herself desperately trying to accumulate the money needed to get her family out of Germany when she and my father met. Henry could assume that she would not reject him if he took on debt to rescue Curt and Regina. For her part, my mother did not chafe under my father's wish to make the decisions, as Goldie apparently had, because she was ready for somebody to lift that burden from her shoulders. It was not a marriage of convenience but a union of two people who could understand each other, my grandmother's fondest wish for her son in far-off America.

My father probably wanted to shield my mother from learning that he had a serious relationship right after he left New York. My parents had parted with no commitments to each other at the end of 1939 and she never visited him in Lincoln when he was a bachelor. As such, his relationship with Goldie was above board. The relationship had been over for close to two years when my father returned to New York, wooed my mother, and wed her in just a few weeks. But he may have worried even years later that my mother might be jealous if she read the letters.

Once I realized the letters disclosed the "affaire with Goldy," as my grandmother called it, I began to wonder if my mother had read the letters during the 13 years they were in her possession. Whatever hurt they might have caused, I suspect she would have told me and decided it was too long ago to worry about. She knew her husband loved her deeply. On a subsequent visit to Lincoln for the unveiling of my mother's headstone, I walked around the Jewish cemetery and discovered that the graves of Goldie's parents are just a stone's throw from my parents' burial plots. They have a lot to talk about.

An Uneasy Homecoming

Unlike my father, my mother returned to visit her hometown after World War II. It was easier to do than for him because she had lived in what became part of the Federal Republic of Germany (West Germany), which was open to tourism. I remember her talking about how much her little town had grown over the decades. It now had parking meters and at least one traffic light. My father joked about her "big city" background even though Großröhrsdorf was much larger than Öhringen.

Despite misgivings based on her history in the town, she made the trip because she wanted to visit her mother's grave in the Jewish cemetery, which had survived the Nazis. My father, of course, had no such graves to visit. She also had somewhat happier memories than he did. Still, despite meeting old Öhringen friends who beseeched her to stay with them and have meals together, she could not make herself spend even one night in the town. At the end of the day, they drove to the Swiss border and never again set foot in what had been their homeland.

My wife and I visited Öhringen while my mother was still alive in 1979. During our stay, we went to my grandmother's grave in the tiny but well-maintained Jewish cemetery surrounded by a high chain-link fence that required keyed entry. We were also able to visit the butcher boy's family who still owned the store and ran the business just across the road from what had been the Rothschild house. The son who had nobly sneaked food to the Rothschilds after dark was now a grown man but did not speak English. His granddaughter had learned English in school, and they took us around town.[8]

Although we enjoyed the experience, I couldn't quite get the Nazis out of my mind. That reality came crashing down on us when we were preparing to leave town. The butcher's wife, who seemed to be channeling my mother, insisted that we could not leave without providing us a to-go package of fresh fruit. Even though they had already fed us well, she insisted on it and asked us to wait in their apartment above the shop. We dutifully walked up the stairs and entered a comfortable family room. I wandered toward the mantelpiece over the fireplace to look at the family photos lined on it, hoping to see an image of the man as the boy who sneaked food to my mother at night.

As I scanned the framed prints, my eyes alit on a portrait of a young man wearing the World War II uniform of the German army. The swastikas on his uniform screamed out to me. I recognized that this was indeed the same man who had hosted us that day, who in his youth had courageously smuggled food to his Jewish neighbors in defiance of the Nazis. I could

---

8. I learned later from his grandson Uli that the butcher we met was Hermann Förnzler, one of two brothers who worked at the butcher shop. It's possible that his slightly younger brother Albrecht might have been the one to smuggle the food to my mother.

barely speak. I motioned for my wife to come over and see. We looked at each other with expressions of shock and dismay. Out of all young men, after having defied the Nazis, how could he have served their cause?

When he and his wife came upstairs with the package of food, I felt embarrassed and disoriented. I tried to look at his face, but my eyes kept darting over to the wartime portrait on the shelf. We clumsily made our excuses, took the bag of fruit with thanks, and hurried off to our car. As we drove to our next destination, trying to process what we had seen, I wondered if my mother had seen the same portrait during her visit and what she thought of it. Perhaps that is why she insisted on leaving town earlier than planned.

A few years later, when controversy arose in the United States over Confederate war memorials, I thought more about the meaning of the man's portrait in his Nazi garb. He wore the uniform of the regular German army, the Wehrmacht, which had been altered with the addition of the Nazi symbols. Had his uniform been adorned with the symbols of the SS, the most vicious and committed of the Nazis, I would have written him off as a hypocrite or opportunist despite his good behavior in the past. In the absence of such evidence, I believe that this man, who lived in a small town, responded to his country's leaders when they called him to arms. That's what young men from small towns have done throughout the ages.

Considering his decency toward his Jewish neighbors before he joined the army, I think it's likely that the young man acted as honorably as a German soldier could while defending his homeland. If he had been ashamed of his service, I doubt the portrait would have been displayed in what was probably the most public room of his apartment. That realization prompted me to write an op-ed column for my local newspaper, the *Gainesville Sun*, arguing that memorials to dead Confederate soldiers were not morally objectionable provided they did not defend or glorify the Southern cause.[9] My column prompted a fellow faculty member to thank me for the sentiments I'd expressed. A draftee in the US Army during the Vietnam War, he appreciated the sharp distinction I'd drawn between honoring individuals for serving, as he had, and praising the cause for which men like him were forced to fight.

Given my predilection to think badly of Germans, I wondered if my father would have approved of this distinction. I was relieved many years later to

---

9. Kenneth D. Wald, "South Carolina Must Honor the Memory, but not the Cause," *Gainesville Sun*, January 22, 2000.

read Norbert's assessment of how my father felt about the subject. Based on his interviews with two of the German POWs whom my father interrogated in Europe, Norbert offered a judicious opinion about my father's attitude toward the ordinary German soldiers he interrogated:

"Henry Wald ... did not appear to them as a superior victor or even hateful, but as a person who benevolently helped the afflicted when it was possible," Norbert said. "And he seems to have made a clear distinction between those who were causally involved in the crimes of the Nazi dictatorship and those who were simply involved in the system as ordinary people."

Even though I know more about the experiences of the Schönwalds than the Rothschilds, I met more of my mother's family during my childhood. We made occasional trips to New York to visit my mother's sister and family, and they came to visit us in Lincoln and Florida for family events. I have interacted much more with my Rothschild cousins than with the Schönwald clan.

My mother's Uncle Sam was the only member of my Rothschild grandparents' cohort whom I met face-to-face. He visited us in Lincoln once and I recall he always wore a bowtie. He loved to play cards with my brother and me and cheated without hesitation, beaming an angelic expression at us when we protested. He spoke almost no English and we knew only German swear words, so there wasn't much verbal communication. I remember him sitting at the kitchen table gazing out the window and across the road at the trains that rumbled by several times each day, very carefully counting the number of cars they hauled. When we took him to a baseball game, he opined that the pitcher must not be very good because he seldom hit the sticks (bats) that the other players were holding.

My circle of Rothschild relatives expanded considerably during my research. Unlike Leo and daughter Lenore Rothschild, whom I had previously discovered thanks to my mother's offhand comment, descendants of this new crop of Rothschild kinfolk have welcomed me into their family. Meeting them reassured me that I was not alone.

I learned about these family ties in 2021 only because my childhood friend Eileen asked me about my family's original name in Germany. She had a school friend with the surname Grunewald whose family had emigrated from Germany to the United States around the same time as my parents. Could the timing and our truncated Wald name mean we were related to her friend?

I told her that we were Schönwalds, not Grunewalds, so there was little chance of that. My mother did have a first cousin in Germany named Hans Grünewald. My mother had once said that she and Hans were quite close in their youth, and she intimated there were romantic sparks between them despite their status as first cousins.

After surviving the war in England, where he was ordained, Hans Grünewald returned to Germany to become Chief Rabbi of Bavaria. My parents visited him in Munich during their only return trip to Germany. In a family of businessmen, he was the only intellectual I knew about, so I hoped for a connection. When I was living in London from 1973–1974, I planned to visit Munich and contacted the rabbi to see if we could meet but received no reply. On returning to London, I found a letter from him informing me that he was visiting his son in London while I was trying to see him in Munich!

Even though there was little likelihood that "our" Grünewald was one of Eileen's friend's Grunewalds, I was intrigued enough to search the web for more information about Cousin Hans. As expected, there was nothing to suggest a tie to Eileen's friend. But Google brought up a link to a family web page created in Potomac, Maryland, by a man named Ralph Grunewald. He mentioned that his father's first cousin was the former Chief Rabbi of Bavaria – none other than Hans Grünewald. He had several photos of Hans visiting his father in the United States and Germany and an audio recording of one long conversation. The man in Ralph's photos was a dead ringer for the Hans Grünewald who was photographed meeting my parents.

Through Ralph, who I think is my third cousin, I've met a slew of new relatives and reconnected with Hans Grünewald's son, himself a prominent English rabbi until he recently retired to Israel. Rabbi Grünewald the younger solved the mystery about how the Rothschild family tree sprouted a Grünewald branch. My maternal grandfather had not only the two brothers, Sam and the aforementioned Leo, but also a sister Julie. She married Edmund Grünewald and took his name. Julie gave birth to Hans. Sadly, she and her husband were deported from their home in Frankfurt and murdered in the Lodz Ghetto.[10]

Despite the tragic ending, finding this flourishing family elated me. Ralph

---

10. List of Murdered Jews from German Federal Archives, *Victims of Persecution of Jews under the National Socialist Tyranny in Germany 1933–1945*, accessed July 30, 2021, from United States Holocaust Memorial Museum, "Holocaust Survivors and Victims Database."

Grunewald and I have so many common interests and experiences that we might have been identical twins separated at birth – despite the inconvenient fact that I'm about six years older. I feel like I've been adopted by the Grunewald clan and will work hard not to sully the family name.

A few weeks after my Öhringen visit, I noticed a small article in the *International Herald Tribune*. It reported that graves in the Jewish cemetery of Ihringen had been defaced. I assumed this was an alternate spelling for my mother's hometown, but it turned out to be a different municipality in the same part of Germany. It was telling that I assumed it was my mother's hometown.

8 LIFE IN LINCOLN

My parents left Casper in 1946 for the somewhat greener pastures of Lincoln where they lived the rest of their lives. With a tenuous grasp of American geography, most people don't know what to say when I tell them I was born and raised in Nebraska. They usually get a puzzled look on their faces, fumble around for something to say, and end up telling me that it must be very cold there. I think they confuse it with Alaska, the other state ending with those four letters.

My fellow Jews have an even harder time processing my exotic background as part of the Nebraska Diaspora. On being told that I am a Cornhusker, many blurt out in astonishment or disbelief, "There are Jews in Nebraska?" A few ask me if I know their friend or acquaintance who lives there on the assumption that all Nebraska Jews know one another – which we kind of do. Because of my origins, I've never won a single round of "Jewish Geography." That's a game that begins when two newly acquainted Jews ask each other about their geographical history and compare notes about common acquaintances. It concludes when they discover they are cousins.

My grandparents were equally vague about Midwestern geography. When my father told my grandfather about planning to relocate from Lincoln to Casper, my grandfather expressed some concern about moving to what he called "Indian country." He worried that the move could delay correspondence about their visas.

My father had a story about how he got from New York to Lincoln that I desperately hope is true. He first lived in the Washington Heights section, also known as "Frankfurt on the Hudson" because so many German Jewish refugees settled there. Yet even surrounded by other, probably equally compulsive German Jews, my father felt like an outsider. He truly hated cities for their noise, dirt, traffic, and crowding and had trouble finding and holding a job when he first arrived. So, he told me one day, he resolved to move someplace else.

Not having any connections or plans, he simply walked into an office run by a Jewish organization, probably HIAS (Hebrew Immigrant Aid Society). He told the person at the front counter that he wanted to move out of New York. When she asked where he wanted to go, he told her he had no idea but just wanted to leave the city as soon as possible.

She directed him to a large map of the United States on the wall. She told him to close his eyes and pick a spot. He followed her instructions and his fingertip landed on Charlotte, North Carolina. This being the 1940s, and the woman probably considering the South as inhospitable for Jews, she suggested he try again. On the second go, he hit Council Bluffs, Iowa, just across the Missouri River from Omaha, Nebraska.

The woman said the organization didn't have any sponsors in that area, but she knew of a businessman in nearby Lincoln who encouraged Jewish immigrants to relocate there, promising them a job and help in finding housing. That sounded good, so my father followed Horace Greeley's advice and headed West.

The Lincoln where he arrived in 1940 had proportionately about as many Jews as the German hometown he left. The estimated 1,200 Jews in Lincoln in 1940, a whopping 0.09 percent of the population, had two congregations and a Jewish cemetery, but no Jewish community center. As was the custom, the earliest Jewish arrivals established a cemetery upon arriving in 1886 and 20 years later set up a federation – a social welfare organization that raised money for indigents among them. There was no recognizably Jewish neighborhood, although several Jewish-owned wholesale and retail businesses dotted the central business district. None of the K–12 schools I attended had more than a handful of other Jewish students. When I attended the University of Nebraska in the late 1960s, there was no Hillel house, nor do I recall any academic courses about Jews or Jewish student organizations beyond two small fraternities and a sorority. There were few Jewish professors, only one of whom I remember as engaged in communal activities, and a sprinkling of professionals. Most of the Jewish men and women owned, ran, or worked for family-owned businesses catering to the general public.

The generous benefactor who brought my father to Lincoln was a very small man who was larger than life. Dan Hill arrived in the United States from Russia in 1906. Starting as an itinerant peddler of housewares, he graduated to become a small-time dealer in scrap metal, founding the Northwestern Junk and Iron Company a year later. Though the company was eventually renamed more grandly as Northwestern Metals, the modest Hill described himself unashamedly as a junkman. He built one of the largest scrap metal companies in the Midwest that, in time, became a major national center for metal recycling. Active in Lincoln's Jewish community, Hill was eager to expand the local Jewish population. He sponsored the dozen or so Holocaust survivor families who became our family's principal social circle in Lincoln.

The transition to Lincoln was not particularly smooth, as shown by one story. Reinhard Gebler, the unofficial archivist for the Schönwalds in Großröhrsdorf, contacted my father in 1985 to offer him some family memorabilia.[1] Compared to the friends he had left behind, Herr Gebler said, "I am sure that a comforting phase of your life began with your departure from here." My father was eager to correct that misimpression by replying that "the years since 1938 have in no way been calm."[2]

New York had been a challenge, and the adjustment to Lincoln was not easy. In the two or so years he lived in Lincoln before relocating temporarily to Wyoming, my father had three different addresses. He subsequently had three different military postings in the United States and likely several different temporary assignments during his time in Europe. On returning from military service, he went back to Wyoming but finally ended his vagabond phase by settling permanently in Lincoln.

There must have been some delay in connecting with the Hill business because the 1940 census listed my father's occupation as a busboy. Just a week or two after he arrived, his parents noted that they were imagining him in a white uniform manning an espresso machine at the well-known Cornhusker Hotel restaurant. He probably held other part-time positions considering he claimed working 54 hours in the week before the census. Given that my father's culinary skills were limited to pouring a packet of dry soup mix into a pot of boiling water and stirring, I wasn't persuaded by the claim. Then again, who would brag about being a busboy? He lost that job by April 1940.

---

1. Letter from Reinhard Gebler to Henry Wald, September 30, 1985.
2. Letter from Henry Wald to Reinhard Gebler, December 4, 1985.

He told us about working in the kitchen at the Cornhusker in downtown Lincoln when we dined there on some family occasion years later. He launched into a dissertation reminiscent of Sheldon Cooper in "The Big Bang Theory," boring his friends with little-known facts. My father's responsibilities included making the melba toast that always appeared on the bread plate at the hotel restaurant. He had to feed day-old bread into a slicing machine with razor-sharp blades. Because the machine was eager to grab an operator's finger or two, he was lucky to emerge with all his digits attached. This may have seemed like a menial job, but it ranked above other options like dishwashing, which one of my father's German schoolmates described in a 1946 letter as "the traditional profession for all travelers to America."

The letters my father wrote to his parents suggested that he was employed at Northwestern Iron and Metal Company by May 1940.[3] In what his parents took for a good sign about his prospects, he accompanied his boss on a road trip to Kansas City where they sold their scrap to various dealers. About a year and a half later, he was promoted to managing a Northwestern subsidiary in Casper. Judging by a photo of the small building that housed the Casper Pipe and Supply Company, it may not have been much of a promotion. His father congratulated him on his advancement but regretted that my father would have to move to the boondocks. Casper had a population of around 18,000, less than a fifth of Lincoln's. As a novelist of the American Southwest once wrote about an isolated town like Casper, it was surrounded by about a billion acres of nothing. Lincoln must have seemed like a bustling metropolis in comparison.

Ultimately, Hill and his brother Nathan became my father's patrons. When my father was trying to raise money for his parents to come to the United States, he turned to the Hills for a loan. They readily agreed to it, prompting my grandmother to tell her son that it was a sign they had confidence in him. I don't doubt that, but I think it was more their innate kindness to a fellow Jew in distress. They may also have provided the essential affidavits of financial support.

Dan Hill was a man of contradictions. In 1941, an admiring profile in the right-wing *Omaha World-Herald* labeled him accurately as "Lincoln's

---

3. His registration for the military draft, dated October 16, 1940, listed the company as his employer. As further confirmation, the privately published city directory of 1941 listed his occupation as bookkeeper.

Socialist-Capitalist."[4] Hill had joined the socialist movement as a young man in Russia and ran for Congress under its banner in 1932.

He did not abandon his beliefs as he became a prosperous business owner and major employer. In fact, as his grandson Gary told me, Hill insisted his employees form a union. When they protested that he already provided more generous pay and benefits than other employers in Lincoln, he repeated his advice to unionize because "you can't trust the bosses." Their retort: "But Mr. Hill, you're the boss," did not prompt him to change his stance. Because of his progressive economic views, he became a trusted adviser on industrial affairs to various New Deal government leaders, always impressing on them the need for a generous wage scale, unemployment insurance, Social Security, limited work hours, and overtime pay. Astonishingly, the Central Labor Union in Lincoln, affiliated with the American Federation of Labor, named Hill – a wealthy industrialist! – as its representative to the National Recovery Administration.[5]

It was easy to underestimate Hill. Because he was small, spoke with a pronounced Eastern European accent, and had a limited education, I assumed he was neither sophisticated nor cosmopolitan. Yet on reading his correspondence, I discovered an articulate man who wrote strong, clear English prose and argued with nuance and subtlety. Even though he was a pillar of the local Jewish community, his letters to his daughter revealed him to be less than Orthodox in his Judaism. He repeatedly insisted that he was not a religious man and told his daughter in language redolent of Thomas Jefferson that the task of Jews was to "carry on the torch of light and truth and goodwill among men."[6] He followed that mandate with numerous acts of benevolence and philanthropy. Were all Jews as unreligious as Hill, his rabbi declared sardonically at Hill's funeral in 1967, "the future of our Jewish community would be secure."[7]

Socialist or not, religious or not, Mr. Hill, as I still must refer to him, was venerated in our (Republican) home. Once he was invited to dinner. Even though my mother was a consummate cook and hostess, it was the only social occasion when I saw her visibly nervous. My brother and I were

---

4. Elizabeth Hughes, "Lincoln's Socialist-Capitalist," *Omaha World Herald*, March 15, 1942.
5. Letter, Ernest Bock, Lincoln Central Labor Union, to Hugh Johnson, NRA Administrator, *The Papers of Dan Hill, 1882–1967* [privately printed], March 3, 1934. My thanks to Gary Hill for sending me a copy of this material.
6. Letter from Dan Hill to Ghita Hill, *Dan Hill Papers*, June 17, 1947.
7. Harold Stern, "Eulogy for Dan Hill," *Dan Hill Papers*, 1967.

instructed to say nothing beyond greeting our honored guest unless he specifically asked a question. I was surprised we were invited to the dinner because everything had to be perfect. Had something gone awry, however, I'm sure he was the kind of guest who would have overlooked it. In our community, "Dan Hill" was the answer Jews gave when somebody asked them to define a "mensch."[8] He was responsible not just for my family but for the entire group of survivors in Lincoln. I think I was given the middle name of Dan in tribute to this remarkable man.

Members of Jewish communities in small cities were especially tightly bound to one another during the 1950s and 1960s. Our subcommunity of survivor families exhibited even more solidarity because of our parents' common histories. There were differences among them, to be sure – some had been refugees from Nazi Germany, others were hidden in Russia, and some were survivors of concentration camps elsewhere in Europe. One family arrived with three generations intact, a demographic rarity. The husband of one couple was an Auschwitz inmate who survived the initial selection process that sent most new arrivals immediately to the gas chambers. In Lincoln, these immigrants socialized together, argued loudly about many things, spoke to one another daily by phone, and kept tabs on each other and their children. Our lives revolved around the synagogue, and my parents' few non-Jewish friends were neighbors or clients.

As far as I know, none of the survivors told their children much about their European experiences. Far from being unusual, this reticence was the norm. Years later, when I asked one camp survivor why she and others didn't let their children know about their history, she replied there were two reasons: They didn't want to scare us and they didn't think people were particularly interested in hearing about it. As a friend and contemporary of mine put it, "These parents were doing the best they could to make our lives as normal as possible."[9] The Lincoln Jewish community, like many others, did not emphasize the Shoah (the Hebrew word for Holocaust) until NBC broadcast a 1978 television miniseries based on Gerald Green's novel. By then, most of us had grown up and moved away.

At some level, I think we children of survivors knew there was something "off" about our parents. Granted, all kids probably think their parents are crazy, but children of immigrant survivors may have had even more reason to think that about parents who spoke with accents, ate strange food, and

---

8. A Yiddish term for a good man, a person of rectitude.
9. Eileen Sommerhauser Putter, "Something Unique is Happening," February 2019, unpublished essay,

didn't care much about baseball or football. Our parents' decision to suppress their memories may have been good for those of us in the second generation, but the survivors paid a price for keeping their emotions bottled up. At a time when Jews had extremely low rates of suicide, there were several among the survivor community in Lincoln.

I've already mentioned my father's survivor guilt. My mother had at least two emotional breakdowns related to her German experiences and, when war loomed in Israel in June 1967, she told me that it was the Holocaust all over again. Perhaps that's why I emptied my modest bank account to support the Israel emergency campaign of the United Jewish Appeal. In 1990, I received a phone call from my brother while I was living in Israel as a Fulbright professor at the Hebrew University of Jerusalem. As war with Iraq neared, he told me, our mother was terrified that we would all be gassed by Iraqi planes dropping chemical weapons. She couldn't deal emotionally with the prospect of losing more family members to poison.

As children of immigrants, my brother and I were encouraged above all else to pursue education, the ultimate portable resource. I suspect the girls we grew up with may have heard differently from their parents, but they were no less diligent in their studies or ambitious for good lives. Even compared to our Jewish friends whose parents had not experienced the Holocaust, we stood out for our academic drive. Sports and social lives were acceptable diversions only as long as our grade-point averages did not suffer.

I don't remember ever "deciding" to go to college. There was nothing to decide. It was as natural a life step as walking, learning to drive a car, or getting married. I can only imagine how my parents would have howled with astonishment had I even hinted at the concept of a "gap year." We should achieve the academic heights, we understood, but not act in a way that would rile up the Gentiles.

There is a classic story about a Jewish mother pushing a stroller with her two infant boys. When an admirer asked her the names of the children, she gestured to them and answered, "That one is the doctor and the other one is the lawyer." The story was not based on my brother and me but could have been. After a brief flirtation with the idea of becoming a rabbi, Steve became fascinated with science and chose medicine as his career. He became, as he never failed to remind me, a "real" doctor. He was a prominent pediatric neurosurgeon who spent most of his career in academic medicine.

As a brain surgeon, he won our fraternal competition hands-down to be the favored son, although I launched a long-running campaign to persuade him that our mother liked me more. We had great fun with this mock feud. When I learned that the Unabomber had been reported to law enforcement by his younger brother and mother, I spoke of the Unabomber's family members as my role models. I even dummied up a fake letter to Steve from the FBI, reporting that it had investigated him because his mother and brother had also denounced him to the authorities. I sent him a fake newspaper ad announcing a new series of tapes in which my mother acknowledged she'd always liked me more.[10]

I majored in political science, thinking I would then get a law degree, but was seduced into an academic career. I knew I was to some extent living a life to fulfill my parents' wishes but never resented it because my life and work were so fulfilling. I appreciated the freedom to choose my career instead of being pressured to join my father's business, but my brother and I eventually concluded that my father doubted we were smart enough to run his accounting practice.

My father's favorite aphorism, "Don't break your arm patting yourself on the back," said it all. After falling short of any goal, we were discouraged from explaining our failure with any sentence beginning with "if." When we broke that rule, he was sure to trot out another old German saying, "If my grandmother had wheels, she'd be a bus." That ended the conversation because we had no idea how to respond.

Whatever we accomplished, I learned, should be enjoyed but not celebrated in an unseemly or flashy way. Above all else, we should do nothing that would stoke resentment from our non-Jewish acquaintances, a lesson both parents drew from their experiences under the Third Reich. My father showed us how to follow that path in 1966 when authors Nelly

---

10. I uncovered evidence that resorting to humor in the face of family conflict is a genetic predisposition passed down from our ancestors, my grandfather and great-uncle in particular. The smoking gun, as it were, was a poem written by Lothar Schönwald to poke fun at his older brother, Curt, on the occasion of the latter's forthcoming marriage in 1909. Lothar described his older brother as a troublemaker, a real handful who was nonetheless beloved by the family, especially his mother. In the presence of Regina, then Curt's fiancée, Lothar poetically recounted a story about how his brother entered a room where she was sleeping and rolled himself into a carpet, presumably to surprise her. On waking, she ignored the carpet, leaving Curt sweaty and short of breath until he could escape. Regina was not amused. Had anything equivalent happened during my brother's courtship of his wife, I would have missed no opportunity to embarrass him about it in public. The poem is *"Zur Hochzeitsfeier seines lieben Bruders Curt Schönwald mit Fräulein Regina Zadek gewidmet von Lothar Schönwald,"* Zittau, November 18, 1909.

Sachs and S. Y. Agnon received the Nobel Prize for literature for their powerful stories evoking the lost world of Eastern European Jews.

My father called the *Lincoln Journal*, our local newspaper, to complain vociferously when he saw the headline about Sachs and Agnon in the evening edition: "Two Jews Get Nobel Award."[11] By the next morning, possibly due to my father's wrath, the story was relabeled "Two Jewish Authors Win Nobel Jointly."[12] My father considered the original headline unseemly, likely to incite envy among non-Jewish readers. It's also possible my father had so often heard "Jew" as a sneering insult in Germany that he wanted to avoid the term altogether, preferring "two Jewish authors." It was acceptable for a Jewish newspaper like the *Forward* to identify the authors as "two Jews," as it did in its headline, but a publication that circulated among a general audience needed to be more circumspect.

Loyalty to the tribe meant avoiding acts that brought shame to the family or community. Even changing one's name to sound less Jewish and more American – say from Myron to Mike – was disdained by my parents as an assault on communal integrity. We were also policed by the "Daily Record," a section in the *Lincoln Journal*. It listed the name of every individual who was involved in legal action in city and county courts. Speeding tickets, shoplifting, bankruptcies, criminal indictments, divorces – they were all there in agate type. Read avidly, it was a precursor to today's social media shaming sites.

Jews, particularly survivors, apparently combed through it to identify and shame the miscreants in their midst, bringing the same energy to the task that they would to parsing the Talmud. Having one's name in agate type was like wearing Hester Prynne's scarlet A because it advertised bad behavior by Jews – or people with Jewish-sounding names – to the Gentile readership in Lincoln.

The section occasionally snared people named Wald. My parents and brother were menaces on the road, and my mother was particularly dangerous to herself and innocent pedestrians, more so as she grew older. Knowing her aversion to bad publicity, my father's partner negotiated a deal in which she surrendered her driver's license and the police officer who ticketed her for her most recent accident dropped the charges. She paid a high price, but at least nobody would learn of the shameful traffic infraction

---

11. "Two Jews get Nobel Award," *Lincoln Journal*, October 20, 1966, 10.
12. *Lincoln Star*, October 21, 1966

from the newspaper. If Jews do indeed feel guilty about everything, you can credit growing up in a culture built on shame.

The mothers in our social group were especially proficient at monitoring the behavior of their offspring. Through phone calls, coffee klatches, mahjong games, and other means, they created a surveillance state that any dictator would have envied. If you did something wrong that escaped the notice of the newspaper, it would soon become semi-public knowledge in their private network.

I was reminded of the global reach of this network when I told my mother that I had leased an apartment in Jerusalem for the upcoming term as a Fulbright professor in Israel. "I know," she calmly told me. I asked how she knew something I had done across five time zones just a few hours earlier. The source was one of her friends, the mother of a lawyer who had immigrated to Israel and whom I had asked to review the Hebrew language lease.

A Jew anywhere who brought shame on the community put Jews at risk everywhere. Conversely, my parents said, Jews should take *quiet*, collective pride in the accomplishments of other Jews. My mother once peculiarly expressed this norm. On November 22, 1963, the day President Kennedy was assassinated, I came home from middle school to find my mother virtually catatonic. She was pale and could barely speak. When I came in through the door, she looked at me and said that now it would happen: We would be blamed, and they would come for us.

I knew instantly who "we" and "they" were. She spent the next few days anxiously looking out the window as if expecting a Gestapo unit to be massing outside our door and rounding us up for deportation. Days later, when Lee Harvey Oswald, the assassin, was shot and killed by a small-time Jewish gangster from New Orleans, she was relieved. Maybe now, she said, we would be okay because a Jew had avenged America.

I don't want to exaggerate. My parents loved Lincoln. Although we encountered some antisemitism, it was more a nuisance than a threat. For example, after a minor quarrel, the crazy woman who lived next door posted a handwritten sign in her garage window that faced our side door. It read, "This property is under the authority of the Nazi Party" and was graced by a swastika in a poorly drawn circle. My mother was alarmed, no doubt, but relieved when the other neighbors who heard about it rushed over to apologize and assure her they didn't share the sentiment. Most of them, I think, had run-ins with the same neighbor who had a German-sounding last name. I'm sure my mother slept better when the woman moved away.

My mother said she liked Lincoln because the people didn't wear their religion on their sleeves. I think she meant that being Jewish was not seen as a mark of the devil but as a respectable religious preference.

In his study of Holocaust survivors, the sociologist William Helmreich argued that most of them built successful lives in the United States.[13] He meant that they managed to go about their days in a relatively ordinary way. On the surface, at least, they succeeded in building a normal environment for their children. Some, of course, could not function normally and turned to destructive behavior that passed their trauma on to the next generation. All survivors were in some way marked by their experiences, but it didn't dominate their lives.

My brother and I knew we were loved and enjoyed a functional family. As we grew up, we came to see our parents as ordinary people who had conquered extraordinary circumstances. I suspect that most of us raised in survivor families still measure ourselves against our parents and remain unsure that we could match the survival skills they demonstrated every day.

---

13. William Helmreich, *Against All Odds: Holocaust Survivors and the Successful Lives They Made in America*, second edition (New York: Routledge, 2017), 6.

PART 3
THE AFTERLIFE OF MY GRANDPARENTS

9 UNEXPECTED VOICES

Barely a month after returning from my first visit to Großröhrsdorf in 2000, while the Schönwald letters were still being translated into English, I received an unexpected email from one of its residents:

July 12, 2000

Dear Mr. Dr. Wald,

We've been searching for you intensively for three years. But we didn't know your exact name.

My name is Norbert Littig. I was born in 1956. I studied theology. During my studies, I became aware of the high amount of injustice [guilt] the theological antisemitism is to blame for. Religion, Jewry and Israel were taboos in the time of the GDR [East Germany]. Under the roof of the church there were Christian-Jewish study groups working for understanding and getting over this dark part of German history.

I'm a Protestant pastor in Grossroehrsdorf/Kleinroehrsdorf and together with two friends Mr. Eckhard Hennig – a teacher in pension [retired] – and Mr. Matthias Mieth – an architect – I've been trying hard to find "tracks" of the Schönwald family.

We interviewed many witnesses of that time and searched archives so we could collect valuable material [pictures and texts]. Because of my work as a teacher for Religious Education at High School also many students [10th grade] collaborated. Our school has got an exchange school in Herzlia/Israel. In the archive of Yad Vashem we learnt about the death of your grandparents in Trawniki near Lublin in 1942.

We were acquainted with Reinhard Gebler and appreciate his historical work for Grossroehrsdorf. We knew he was a friend of the Schönwalds and he corresponded with your father Heinz Schönwald. He himself pointed the Jewish origin of the textile store in Grossroehrsdorf out to me. ...

In 1998, commemorating Kristallnacht 60 years ago, we intended to publish a fictitious interview with Curt Schönwald. ... Our mayor ... Eckert refused to publish it in the local paper ... so it was published in another newspaper.[1] Many inhabitants of Grossroehrsdorf thanked us and encouraged us to work on.

Yours,

Norbert Littig, with kind regards to your family

This email stunned and elated me. When we visited in 2000, nobody in Großröhrsdorf had said anything about the ongoing efforts by Norbert and his friends to recover my family's German history. I raced to show the message to Robin and shared it with all my family members.

The message arrived at the perfect moment. I was ready to learn more about my family. Psychological connections had been established, but I still had lingering questions and doubts. On my visit in 2000, I asked indelicately why a family that had given so much to the town was treated so shabbily. Several people told me that none of the locals participated in Kristallnacht, that ringing the church bells did not bring forth neighbors to aid in the attack, and that the leaders of the riot were outsiders imported from Dresden.

I appreciated hearing this message and learning about the respect that townspeople showed my grandparents, but I did not entirely believe it. I knew that Germans in many small towns were deeply ashamed of their role as bystanders and invented a past where Nazi efforts against local Jews

---

1. Eckhard Hennig, Matthias Mieth, Norbert. Littig, "*Warum läuteten vor 60 Jahren, am 9. November, die Glocken in Großröhrsdorf?*" *Ausgabe Kamenz-Süd*, November 7, 1998, 13–14. The article also appeared on page 11 of the *Sächsische Zeitung* on the same date.

were met by widespread resistance and noncompliance. For all the expressions of goodwill that greeted me, I doubted that Großröhrsdorf was any different.

I told Norbert that I welcomed his group's interest because I was nagged by thoughts of unfinished business. He later told me he was relieved by my response, thinking I might not want anything to do with the town. Had his message arrived before I had the letters and had visited the town, when I still hated everything to do with Germany, I would probably have dismissed it rudely. By responding positively to his invitation, he wrote, I had "rebuilt the broken bridge to the past" and my family's roots.

When I finally met Norbert, Matthias, and Eckhard face-to-face in Großröhrsdorf in 2004, they seemed like longtime friends. We had already developed a partnership from a distance as we worked to find more traces of my family. I entrusted them with copies of my grandparents' letters to my father and filled in what had happened to the family after 1939. They in turn told me the full story about the family from before 1939 and shared with me a treasure trove of photos, documents, and other items they had uncovered. I did not realize until much later that my curiosity and their outreach would lead eventually to a reconciliation of sorts for me with Germany. Nobody who knew me would have predicted it.

Norbert is a force of nature. A tall man with a lean face and piercing eyes, he calls to mind a prophet from the Hebrew Bible. Given his respect for Judaism, he would consider that description a high honor. As the email indicated, he took on the task of bringing the Schönwald family back to Großröhrsdorf out of a sense of personal moral responsibility.

Although raised in a nonreligious family, Norbert became a Christian as a young man. In East Germany, he would normally have entered the military after completing high school, but his Christian principles wouldn't allow him to take that step. He believed in the righteousness of defending his homeland, he told me, but said that East German soldiers mostly fired their weapons into the backs of other East Germans who were trying to escape to the West. He refused to serve.

The decision cost him a college education. Unable to attend university because he refused military service, he selected the alternative that best suited his Christian beliefs. The regime didn't care about religion, so it allowed conscientious objectors to study in seminaries. At his East Berlin seminary, Norbert learned for the first time about German responsibility for the Holocaust. I was not entirely surprised that he was unaware of it before then because one of the historians from the 2000 Fulbright tour, Thomas C. Fox, told me that East Germany had framed the Holocaust as a Nazi attack on good German communists. Jews were incidental to the story.

While sitting outside a pub one day, I asked Norbert why he had taken on the task of studying my family. Because our language differences made that question difficult to answer in face-to-face conversation, he later sent me a letter of explanation.[2] The quest to reconcile Jews and Germans was personal to him because he saw the Holocaust as the signal failure of Christianity.

"Jesus was a Jew, had lived and believed as a Jew, and it is through Him and His disciples that all the peoples received the message of the love of God," Norbert said. "Thereby God did not 'drop' the Jews. Jews and Christians remain connected in their beliefs in one gracious and merciful God."

He believed that the antisemitism of the German church provided the "breeding ground" for the racialized antisemitism of the Nazis. As he put it concisely in his sermon on the 70th anniversary of Kristallnacht in 2008, "Christians declared Jews as their enemies. This is the biggest cause of the suffering that Jews have been put through at the hands of Christians."[3]

To a practicing Christian like Norbert, every day is a day of atonement. Even under the communist regime of the GDR, he learned Hebrew, studied Jewish traditions, and, after the collapse of communism, joined others in restoring Jewish cemeteries that had been defiled by the Nazis. He agitated for building memorials to the murdered Jews, ensuring that his countrymen would not forget their responsibility for the carnage.

He also took up the quest because it served an important educational function.[4] The Schönwald family's experiences in the period from 1880 to 1945 were typical of German Jewry, he thought, and thus could help his students better understand this "horrible" chapter of German history by making it personal and tangible. Holocaust education in Germany was typically taught from a theoretical perspective that he found sterile. "But when I talk about the example of a specific family that had lived and worked in Großröhrsdorf ... [students] are moved and understand reality

---

2. Letter from Norbert Littig to Kenneth D. Wald, October 4, 2008.
3. Norbert Littig, Memorial Service sermon, "70 Years of Pogrom Night in Großröhrsdorf," November 9, 2008.
4. Letter from Norbert Littig to Kenneth D. Wald, September 7, 2007. A world away, a Holocaust educator in Lincoln reached the same conclusion and adopted our family for pedagogical purposes.

better." Indeed, some of the students in his classes worked on the project directly. He developed exchange partnerships with Jewish schools in Israel as part of that campaign.

The depth of his passion was evident when we talked about the restoration of the Frauenkirche in nearby Dresden. The Church of Our Lady, Dresden's landmark cathedral commonly called the Mother Church, was nearly bombed into oblivion by the American and British air forces near the end of World War II. The first day of the bombing, February 13, 1945, was my birthday, and I used to think the firebombing was a prenatal gift from God. After the war, the church was left in ruins as the East German authorities had neither interest nor funds to rebuild it. When communism fell, a worldwide fundraising campaign provided money for restoration.

As it happens, the topping off of the restored building with a huge cross coincided with my departure from Großröhrsdorf on June 22, 2004. Although he planned to attend the event after dropping me off at the Dresden train station, Norbert regretted the restoration of the cathedral. He told me that Germany had no shortage of Lutheran churches but few places where Germans could confront tangible reminders of the atrocities their country committed. It would have been better, he said, if the church had been left in ruins as a constant reminder of the genocide. I discovered that many German Lutherans – clergy and laypeople alike – shared his view. It is a beautiful cathedral today, but the shards were probably more conducive to serious theological reflection.

Driven by a mission to educate his students and neighbors by making the Holocaust local, he naturally gravitated to the Schönwalds, then (and now) the only Jewish family in town. Starting in 1994, my grandparents became the centerpiece of his research. His supportive wife, Sabine, once said wistfully that she looked forward to "life after Schönwald," which will probably never happen as long as Norbert draws breath. Although he had no formal training in history, Norbert engaged with residents of the town and found a considerable amount of primary material including newspaper advertisements, small favors that my grandparents' store had given out to children, and advertising gifts like a coal shovel with the store logo. He also read everything he could about the fate of Jews in Saxony and corresponded with archivists at Yad Vashem and elsewhere.

He recounted the remarkable discovery of one precious item. While walking through the town one day in 1970, somebody spotted what looked like a piece of scrap metal sticking out of a garbage can. Its faded orange hue and oval shape probably caught the passerby's eye and he retrieved it. It was eventually passed along to Norbert, who recognized it as a sign from the second Kaufhaus Schönwald on Pulsnitzer Street in the 1920s. Battered and scratched, the colorful metal piece still bore the store name in legible print. It became Norbert's icon for our family and the first item to be seen by viewers of the museum exhibit he mounted in 2008. To this day, he has no idea how the sign ended up in the garbage long after the store was demolished. Even as I write these sentences, I can hear some of my friends insisting that the discovery was no accident. Perhaps the sign was a sign.

When I returned to Großröhrsdorf in 2006, for my benefit, Norbert brought together a group of older women who were the younger relatives of store employees. These descendants passed along stories about my grandparents from the older generation. Both the sainted Martha, the family housekeeper known as Frau Martha or Tante [Aunt] Martha, and Hebbor, who cooked and baked, were represented by their nieces. In their long oral history interview, they especially stressed the warmth of my grandparents to their staff and children.

One of the women, Isolde Riss, was the daughter of the store's dresser who designed the window displays and other advertising. At that meeting, she gave me the metal yo-yo that her father had once brought home from work. It has "Kaufhaus Schönwald" on one side and "always cheaper" (in German) on the other. She had played with this toy as a girl and later passed it on to her children. As she put it into my hand, she declared it was time to restore it to the rightful owner. It sits on a shelf in my family room, resting on a small base, covered with a glass dome. It is far too precious to be used as a toy even by my beloved grandchildren. Some years later, her generosity prompted her to give Norbert the tablecloth mentioned in the introduction.

Norbert's two compatriots were also deeply engaged in the act of recovery. Eckhard was a retired history teacher with a personal interest in my family. He remembered when a mob shattered the glass windows of the Schönwald department store during Kristallnacht. True to form, the Nazis did not compensate Jewish business owners for damages from a state-inspired, state-organized riot. In an act that exemplifies the Yiddish term *chutzpah*, authorities forced the Jewish community to pay for repairs to the property and levied a large collective fine for supposedly goading Germans into attacking Jewish property.

My grandfather hired Eckhard's father, a glazier, to replace the windowpanes and duly paid him for the work. Eckhard remembered that his father was then told by the municipality that he was no longer eligible for contract work because he had been employed by "the Jew Schönwald." He had to go hat in hand to the municipality to get back on its list of approved vendors. When he told me the story more than 60 years after it happened, Eckhard's emotions revealed that it felt like yesterday – to both of us.

Matthias, the other member of the group, was an architect who specialized in restoring old buildings. Although he was hired to renovate the Schönwald building for its postwar owners, the Bruckners, his attachment to the family had developed earlier. In a conversation during my 2004 visit, he recounted a conversation with his own father. Matthias was worried about a situation and asked his father what to do. His father told him, "Curt Schönwald will help you." I cannot recall the specifics, but the trust the elder Mieth reposed in my grandfather was what I took away from the conversation.

The building that used to belong to my grandparents had not been damaged in the war but had aged and been neglected under the GDR. Matthias found the original blueprints and documents dating back to the construction of the store in 1928. He made sure that the reborn Kaufhaus was entirely true to its original design. Matthias retained the iconic "Built 1928 CS" that was painted on the exterior. He later gave me a tome with copies of the plans and correspondence that related to the original construction of the store. The last time I visited, the building housed a boutique mall with the upstairs rooms still rented out as apartments. It is a striking building in a town with mostly functional architecture.

Beyond his professional work on the building, Matthias had a personal incentive to join the hunt. He had become a fervent Christian Zionist, joining a small religious congregation in town. Feeling responsibility and remorse for what the town had done to my family, he made multiple pilgrimages to Israel and studied Judaism. In a letter sent shortly after our first meeting, he explained his thinking succinctly: "We are the children of the delinquents ... and you are the son of the martyrs."[5] He identified so strongly with Jewish suffering that I frequently saw him wearing a kippah, the ceremonial head covering worn by religiously observant Jews.

When he dropped me off at my hotel after dinner one night during my 2004 visit, he expounded further on the reasons for his involvement. He said, "I know it is not possible that the Schönwald family will move back to the town, but it is very important that the town learns what it lost when the

---

5. Letter from Matthias Mieth to Kenneth D. Wald, September 4, 2004.

Schönwalds left in 1939." My memory of his words might be hazy, but I can still see his serious face and hear the slight tremor in his voice. We hugged and he drove off. I didn't sleep much that night.

Despite the goodwill I felt from Norbert, his colleagues, and other townspeople, some citizens of Großröhrsdorf had not always welcomed inquiries about their town under National Socialism. Having seen the 1993 German film, "Nasty Girl," a fictional account based on a real event, I was not surprised by their reaction. The film tells the story of a bright young student who entered a contest to write about her small town during the Third Reich. She had been raised on stories about the town's heroic resistance to Nazism.

Through diligent research, she discovers that the town was fully complicit with the regime and that many leading citizens had been Nazi Party members from an early date. They collaborated eagerly in driving out the Jewish residents and confiscating their properties. Stores in the town helped supply the numerous concentration camps in the area, which were an open secret. When denied access to the municipal archives, she won a lawsuit that yielded even more damning information that further undermined the town's carefully constructed image of itself. For challenging the myths that spared the collaborators' guilt, she and her family were harassed, intimidated, and physically assaulted. Her home was fire-bombed, yet she persisted.

Norbert, Eckhard, and Matthias did not encounter resistance nearly on the same scale, but it was clear the authorities felt that paying attention to the Nazi past would hinder efforts to attract foreign investment and shore up the declining textile industry. As Norbert's email reported, the mayor, an ex-communist, forbade the municipal newspaper from printing their fictitious interview with my grandfather in 1998.

The trio persevered with the ultimate goal of persuading the town to erect a monument to the Schönwald family. Instead of denying the Nazi past, they were asking the local council to commemorate it openly in the heart of town. Even though I could not imagine anybody resisting Norbert successfully for any length of time, I doubted the campaign would succeed.

Over the years, Norbert added massively to the material archive I had accumulated from *Herr* Gebler's collection, passed on to me by his grandson, and the various photos and documents my father had saved. Periodically, I received thick envelopes from Norbert that included photos and background information he had discovered. I also began to get more systematic about collecting information. As it had for Norbert when he found the store sign in a rubbish bin, serendipity played a role in my discoveries.

When I searched the catalog of the US Holocaust Memorial Museum in Washington in 2005, I noticed a volume that dealt with Jewish slave laborers in Berlin from 1941–1943. The book was based on a trove of identity cards and personnel information about German Jews who had been forced to work in an electrical factory.[6] I knew the Nazis had enslaved Slavs from the conquered territories of Eastern Europe and used imprisoned Jews in forced labor but was unaware that Jews living in Germany were also conscripted. I found an index entry for "Schönwaldt, Kurt" on page 238.

Despite the differences in spelling of both the first and last names, I found my grandfather staring out from the page. I had no doubt it was him and found independent confirmation when I showed the photocopy to a friend whose first words were "Ken, that's you." There was further proof when I later received my grandfather's file from the Berlin state archives.[7] The Ehrich and Graetz electrical company attested in writing that it had employed one "Kurt Israel Schönwald."[8]

The company that collaborated with the Nazis during World War II made sure to include the middle name of Israel he was forced to carry but couldn't even manage to spell his first name correctly. His monthly earnings would barely have covered his rent, leaving nothing for food, utilities, or other essentials. To add insult to injury, the Berlin Jews were assigned to build armaments for the German war effort. I hope they followed the example of the Jews in *Schindler's List,* who apparently sabotaged the shells they built so they wouldn't work.[9] Nothing about this "employment" made it into the letters he wrote to my father. Calling my grandfather an

---

6. Aubrey Pomerance, *Jüdische Zwangsarbeiter Bei Ehrich & Graetz, Berlin-Treptow* (Cologne: DuMont and the Jewish Museum of Berlin, 2003).
7. The material provided by Frau Dr. Nakath from the Brandenburgisches Landeshauptarchiv in Potsdam was sent on November 7, 2005. It included separate files for Curt, Regina, and Johanna Pless.
8. Ehrich and Graetz AG, *Beecheinigung* [Attestation], March 14, 1942.
9. There is debate about whether the Schindler Jews actually vandalized armaments. For one survivor's views, see "Ludmilla Page Describes Sabotage during Production of Munitions in Oskar Schindler's Factory in Brünnlitz," *Holocaust Encyclopedia,* https://encyclopedia.ushmm.org/content/en/oral-history/ludmilla-page-describes-sabotage-during-production-of-munitions-in-oskar-schindlers-factory-in-bruennlitz.

employee when he was conscripted forcibly is like describing slaves on American plantations as independent contractors.

My elation about finding a new picture of my grandfather was tempered as I looked more closely at the photo. In all the prior photos of my grandfather I'd seen, he struck me as a man of vitality and bristling energy. I am particularly impressed by a photo probably taken by my grandmother during a family vacation in the 1920s in what was called "Saxon Switzerland," a region with mountainous terrain and large hills. My father and Aunt Suse stand on the rocks above an entrance to what looks like a cave, wearing casual clothes and holiday smiles. In contrast, my grandfather stands by the entrance, wearing a suit and tie. His pose – the fearless and determined expression on his face, ramrod posture, and arms folded against his hips as if impatient to get on with it – remind me of a formidable bantam rooster. Despite his small stature, I would not want to tangle with him.

The "Kurt Schönwaldt" pictured in the book was in his early sixties but could easily have been ten years older. Although our basic facial features were similar, his gaunt cheeks, sunken eyes, and threadbare suit testify to the price of hard labor. Even by the standards of a passport picture, which Norbert believes it to have been, my grandfather looked awful.

He was staring away from the camera with a blank expression that could have been confusion, shock, resignation, or studied indifference. He had a bloodless, ghost-like appearance.

In every other portrait I had seen of him, he looked straight into the camera lens with a confident expression. Despite the family resemblance, I would not have recognized him as the handsome and immaculately turned-out gentleman in the portrait that hung on our dining room wall. If I look closely at the low-resolution photograph from his identity card, I think I see the ribbon for the Iron Cross on his lapel. Even in slavery, he was a proud German patriot.

The exhaustion apparent in the photo and his ravaged physical condition made me wonder if he even survived the torturous train journey that soon took him across Europe or his period of internment at the work camp near Trawniki. That concern deepened when I discovered the US government form from June 1942 in which my father told American authorities that his parents had been deported.[10] Referring to the conditions in the Polish labor

---

10. Henry W. Wald, addendum to "Alien's Personal History Statement," submitted to Lancaster County Selective Service Board #1, June 17, 1942.

camps, which were widely known, he said matter-of-factly, "I have reason to believe that my parents may not be alive anymore now since I know that diseases are raging in those areas and besides these people are not being fed by the Nazis." He might have known that the slave laborers were also being killed intentionally by gunfire when they refused to be worked to death.

A librarian at the US Holocaust Museum suggested I contact the state archives in Germany to see if they had additional information about my grandparents. The chances were slim that a state archive would have anything so long after the fact, but it was worth a try.

I knew from experience that Germans did not throw away government documents, although many were destroyed during the Allies' bombing campaign. As young adults in Germany, my father and mother had worked long enough to pay into the German social security fund and were entitled to pensions when they turned 65. Decades later, when they reached retirement age, the pension checks arrived in the mail. My mother also qualified for other reparation programs that required original documentation we obtained. The documents about my grandparents had not been destroyed during the war and the archive eventually provided me with copies.

Even though I admired the bureaucratic efficiency that produced the documents, the Germans could not resist acting in a, well, Germanic manner. When my mother died, I was required to return the last payment she had received from her German pension. Unlike the American system, the German pension laws demanded repayment of the stipend for the month the recipient had heedlessly chosen to die. In a passive-aggressive response that she would have appreciated, I kept the money in an account for nearly a year, hoping it would annoy German authorities. Frequent demands for repayment suggested it worked. I was sorely tempted to pay it off in pennies, but the postage was prohibitive.

Abetted by Norbert's labors, my store of documents grew apace, consuming an ever-increasing amount of shelf space in my study. When I was asked to speak at the local Holocaust remembrance ceremony in Gainesville in 2009, a friend who serves as the videographer came by my house to identify materials for a presentation that would run while the audience was arriving in the synagogue sanctuary. As I showed him the documents and photos I'd acquired, he remarked that I probably knew more about my family's history than any other Jew he knew. I was shocked to realize that I'd learned so much about prior generations of Schönwalds. When I told stories about the family to friends and colleagues, they invariably urged me to write about it. Their comments planted the idea of writing a book. Blame them.

10 FRUITS OF THEIR LABOR

I returned to Großröhrsdorf in 2008, my fourth visit in less than ten years. On this trip, I reaped the fruits that Norbert, Matthias, and Eckhard had sown with their labor of love. As a result, I came to terms with my own views about Germans, realizing as David French once observed that "encountering people in full, rather than as mere online avatars for hated ideas, can indeed soften hearts and change minds."[1]

Against all odds and my skepticism, my three German friends had persuaded the local council to build a memorial to my grandparents. Financed by private donations, the monument sits on a pedestrian island across from the old Schönwald store, tended by Norbert, who sweeps off snow and grime as needed. To help the townspeople better understand the monument's importance, Norbert also completed and published a German book about the Schönwald family.[2]

The book revealed details I hadn't known. It reported the degree to which town officials faithfully implemented Nazi decrees and how the schools became agents of the regime. I also learned that in 1937, my father was arrested for *Rassenschande* [race disgrace] by the state prosecutor – the incident that may have sent him to Sachsenburg. The book also further

---

1. David French, "The Lost Boys of the American Right," *New York Times*, August 13, 2023, https://www.nytimes.com/2023/08/13/opinion/masculinity-right-young-men.html.
2. Norbert Littig, *Erbaut 1928 CS: Erinnerung an die Jüdische Familie Schönwald aus Großröhrsdorf* [Built in 1928 C S. Remembrance of the Jewish Schönwald Family from Grossröhrsdorf], (Großröhrsdorf, Germany, 2008), self-published.

revealed how the Nazis extorted the thriving Kaufhaus Schönwald from my grandparents. Norbert was especially indignant about the racist bookkeeping that discounted the sale price of the building by the outstanding balance on the loan, effectively making it an undeserved gift to Herr Seifert. Norbert reports in agonizing detail how many institutions in the town enlisted eagerly in the Nazi crusade.

Certain images came to mind when I read about the public officials who volunteered to remake Großröhrsdorf as a Nazi city by ignoring the basic principles of justice and law. In 1999, the Jewish Studies program at my university hosted "The Rule of Law," an exhibition by a Miami painter-sculptor who specialized in the Holocaust.[3] To get to it, audiences were supposed to walk on a path composed solely of open-faced law books. The artist told me that some visitors to the exhibition refused to follow directions and circumvented the objects. On reaching the exhibition, they were confronted by a large stack of burned law books that had been impaled on a metal rod and hung from the ceiling on a hook. The slaughterhouse metaphors were inescapable.

Without Norbert's biography, this book could not have been written. The dedication of the monument and book launch were scheduled for November 3–9, 2008, a week commemorating the 70th anniversary of Kristallnacht. The city's cultural center hosted an exhibition of photographs and other items along with explanatory text from Norbert's book. Before the dedication, Norbert gave us a personal tour, translating the German text as best he could.

My brother and his daughter Sarah made their first visit to the town for these events, and I was accompanied by my wife, Robin, and youngest daughter, Jaina. Before I arrived, Norbert gave Steve and Sarah a whirlwind tour of all the locations mentioned in the book. They could barely keep up with him. When my family and I arrived later, he took all of us to the Jews House in Berlin. He boldly knocked on the door of the apartment my grandparents had occupied. The current resident told us he didn't know the history of the flat and, when we asked, said he hadn't come across my father's letters to his parents. They were probably destroyed when my grandparents were forced to turn over their possessions and vacate the premises in 1942. Despite all the materials that were saved, I still mourn the loss of these documents.

---

3. Joe Nicastri, "The Rule of Law," *Past Project*, Bridge Red Studios, North Miami, FL, https://www.bridgeredstudios.com/project_past/13_rol.

Earlier that week, Eckhard and a local woman performed a public reading of my grandfather's letters to my father. It was the first and only time the letters were read publicly in Germany. I didn't arrive in time for the event and wondered how the letters affected the audience.

On Friday, I was to speak on behalf of the family at a public gathering at the cultural center. My comments would be translated into German by Kerstin Schneider, who had assisted Norbert in his research. The talk would be broadcast throughout Saxony by state media. I sent my lecture in advance so Kerstin had time to translate it and ask questions about the meaning of unfamiliar words.

Writing the talk was challenging because of my conflicting emotions and that I was speaking in front of an audience that included members of my family. After thinking about many alternatives, I entitled it simply "Reconciliation." That seemed to encapsulate the meaning of the entire week for our family.

Sunday began with a memorial service at Norbert's church. I was particularly moved by his intercessory prayer that spoke about the Jewish people: "We look upon their suffering with distress, suffering that was forced upon them throughout their long history alongside Christianity. In this week we have come to realize, that in our own town Großröhrsdorf, a Jewish family Schönwald was done a massive injustice. We beg you: Lord, have mercy."[4]

He told his congregants to cherish the opportunity to reconcile with the family that had been wronged. Rather than dwell only upon past sins, he thanked God for gifting them with a new beginning. Alluding to the Schönwald family's presence in the pews, he rejoiced that "With those that were forced to suffer, we are able to meet again."

He also linked the suffering of the past to the present by speaking about a large refugee camp, which coincidentally was near the municipal baths that my family had helped fund in the 1930s. He reminded his parishioners that the camp was home to others who had been pariahs in their own countries. "In that camp," he said, "there live Iraqi Christians who still speak the language Jesus spoke (Aramaic). There live Armenian Christians from Turkey. In that camp, there are also Muslim refugees and Hindus." He urged the congregation to see the face of Jesus and other Jews in those refugees. I've rarely heard anyone explain so clearly what it means to think

---

4. Norbert Littig, Intercessory prayer for memorial service, November 9, 2008.

globally and act locally. I hope his call to action inspired congregants to reach out to the refugees.

A few hours later, city officials dedicated the monument to my grandparents in a public ceremony near the store. Covered mostly in elegant Jerusalem stone, it displays a photograph of my grandparents and a description of their life in the town, their departure after Kristallnacht, and their deaths. The monument does not look like a typical war memorial. Rather, it resembles the *bimah* on which the Torah is read during Jewish religious services.[5] I am certain this feature was Norbert's doing.

The monument is also unusual in its frankness. The inscription written by Norbert describes what happened to my grandparents in detail:

> Here lived Curt and Regina Schönwald with their children, Heinz and Suse. Since 1928 they had a well-known textile shop. On the night [of November 10, 1938] this shop was damaged by a small group of National Socialists. They destroyed the windows. Curt and Regina had to move away from the city. The oldest inhabitants say, "It was terrible and we are ashamed that we didn't do anything to protest this terrible thing." Heinz and Suse emigrated, but the parents were deported from Berlin in 1942. At this time we can't change what happened, but now we have to remember every day. This is our part, for us and our children. We will remember with this family.

During the ceremony, there was none of the ambivalence that had prompted the ex-communist mayor to prevent the publication of a newspaper column about the Schönwalds just ten years earlier. On the contrary, the new mayor took ownership of their fate on behalf of the town.

In the forthright words of Mayor Kerstin Ternes, the town publicly remembered when "the dignity and the rights of our Jewish citizens were torn to pieces." With "grief and sorrow, horror and shame," she said publicly, the town now recognized its obligation to remember and commemorate the 1938 pogrom by raising the monument. After the memorial was unveiled, my brother led us in reciting the Mourner's Kaddish, the Jewish prayer of remembrance. I told the audience that we finally had a gravesite to visit. We concluded by placing stones on the

---

5. Hebrew for the raised platform on which the table sits.

monument as per the Jewish custom; the citizens of Großröhrsdorf placed flowers around the base.

Norbert refers to these moments as "the Großröhrsdorf apology," an extraordinary time in the town's history. The phrase resonated powerfully with my South African cousin Cal – my grandparents' great-granddaughter who has long been interested in our family's history. She convened a post-apartheid conference at the University of Cape Town in 2014 on the importance of apology in reconciliation.[6] Norbert spoke at the conference in person, explaining the efforts that led up to the pivotal apology, and I participated via Skype (as well as I could at 6 a.m. Florida time). I described what the apology meant to our family and how it changed my perspective on Germany.

As we mingled with the audience after the brief unveiling ceremony, a resident took me aside and handed me a gift box. It contained a small square of concrete and asphalt with an embedded brass plaque. The *Stolperstein* or "stumble stone," as it is known in English, has become a common way to memorialize Jews who died in the Holocaust. Containing information about the individuals and their fate, they are meant to be embedded in the sidewalk outside the homes or offices of Holocaust victims to remind passersby of what was lost in the genocide. These small memorials, found all over the continent, remind me of headstones at a burial site. Although he appreciated the sentiment, Norbert did not like the symbolism of people walking on a memorial and I deferred to his judgment. The Stolperstein now rests on a shelf in my family room. It may not be in the ground, where it was meant to be found, but it is implanted in my memory.

In talks about this experience, I've displayed a photo of the memorial taken by my youngest daughter. I'm usually the photographer in the family but was too occupied to play that role. My daughter, a good photographer, shot several images that captured the reflection of the Kaufhaus Schönwald in the glass that covers the photograph and the story of my grandparents. When I edited one of the photos, I noticed an object in the lower left portion of the glass. I couldn't quite make it out and was on the verge of deleting it from the image. On closer inspection, I realized it was not a random item but a reflection of my daughter's hands on the camera that captured the photo. In a way, my daughter was extending her hand to my

---

6. C. Volks and S. Musungu, "Building Empathy by Watching Apologies: Perceptions of Facilitators Regarding Bystanders and Perpetrators," *South African Journal of Higher Education*, 30 (2016), 112–25, https://doi.org/10.20853/30-4-677.

grandparents across the generations just as they had reached out to me through their letters.

Not everybody was reconciled to the symbolic return of the Schönwalds to the town. A few months after the dedication, the monument was defaced with Nazi slogans. Saxony was a Nazi stronghold during World War II and nearby Dresden has provided a disproportionate share of votes for neo-Nazi parties since the reunification of Germany. So this desecration wasn't unforeseeable. Norbert told me that his family and fellow parishioners worked without interruption to scrub away the slogans and restore the memorial. I have no doubt they achieved that goal.

Despite promising his wife he would turn his time and attention to other subjects once the memorial was dedicated, Norbert has not been able to let go of the Schönwalds. In the summer of 2015, he decided to recreate the trip that took my grandparents from Berlin to Sobibor.[7] He described it as a shattering experience, precisely the reaction I would have expected from a man of such empathy and moral conscience.

He took the train from Berlin to Trawniki and then – like the deportees – walked to the town of Piaski where they were barracked. He could find nothing to commemorate the victims who lived there before their transit to Sobibor where more than a quarter million were murdered. Even near the extermination camp, he found only a small memorial hidden away in a forest. He is now working on another book, the second volume of the Schönwald family history. My cousin and I both contributed chapters about how the Holocaust affected our sides of the family. Norbert wrote a long chapter about my mother's family, an important source for my description of the Rothschilds.

Norbert has become a member of our family and so belongs in this memoir. Deciding that a new generation was a good time to make this status official, we were delighted that Norbert and Sabine could join us for our youngest daughter's New York wedding in 2011. He reminded me that the Jewish wedding ceremony based largely on the Hebrew Bible also provides most of the language for the Christian marriage rite. Jews often chant "We are one" to emphasize our family's feelings toward other Jews. Norbert's expansive vision reminded me that the slogan crosses religious boundaries. I'm glad the Schönwald family is now back in Großröhrsdorf.

---

7. Letter from Norbert Littig to Kenneth D. Wald, February 17, 2016.

11 RECKONING: REVENGE, RECONCILIATION, AND RESPONSIBILITY

Less than a year after the Großröhrsdorf tribute to my grandparents, I delivered the keynote speech at the 2009 Holocaust remembrance ceremony in Gainesville. I asked various friends for suggestions before I composed the lecture for the Großröhrsdorf event. Several of them who served on the planning committee for our community's annual commemoration urged me to speak about my experiences in Germany. We had previously heard mostly from Holocaust survivors or scholars. Because the number of survivors was dwindling, the committee decided it was time to include the impact of the Holocaust on the second generation, the children of survivors sometimes known as 2Gs. My talk was to inaugurate that change.

I decided to talk about the dedication of the monument in Germany and included the lecture I had delivered during the commemoration week in Germany. Never having been good at picking titles, I asked the chair of the event committee – also a child of survivors – for suggestions. Like a good critic, he found a broader theme in my essay than I had recognized. He thought the title should be expanded to "Revenge, Reconciliation, and Responsibility." It was published under that title in 2010 by *Kolot*, a magazine published by the United Synagogue of Conservative Judaism.[1]

As an experienced public speaker, I don't normally read from a text and

---

1. I've added "reckoning" to the title of this chapter because the Gainesville talk was the first time I'd thought about the broader implications of my identification as a child of survivors.

usually rely only on a few notes. I broke that rule for this talk because I knew my emotions would be raw as I spoke to a large room full of friends, colleagues, and family. Talking about my grandparents and parents would test me emotionally.

Some of the statements I made that evening have been superseded by new information. For example, although the official memorial book of Holocaust victims does not report exactly where my grandparents died, the evidence strongly suggests they were killed in Sobibor. Rather than being marched on foot to the local police station during Kristallnacht, as I thought, I learned that they were driven there by car. These details do not change the sentiments I expressed in 2009. I still consider the monument in Großröhrsdorf as my grandparents' tombstone and continue to make progress toward reconciliation.

Speaking from a podium on the bimah of my synagogue, I told the audience how I had ended up on a raised platform in the municipal cultural center of Großröhrsdorf a year earlier. Speaking to a packed sanctuary with overflow seating, I recounted how my family was driven out of that town on Kristallnacht and described the scene when the church bells were rung to summon townspeople to join the small Nazi mob.

I told my Gainesville audience how the vandals rampaged through the store and about my grandfather's arrest, deportation to the Buchenwald concentration camp, and release after three weeks of brutality. I concluded by relating the aftermath – chiefly, my father and his sister's departure from Germany and my grandparents' eventual deportation to Poland.

I then brought the audience up to date about the steps that led me to the podium in Großröhrsdorf following the collapse of East Germany in 1989. Most of that section of my talk focused on Norbert, Matthias, and Eckhard, who in their research discovered that the history of Großröhrsdorf under Nazi rule was the history of the Schönwalds.

I confessed to my Florida audience that I'd had trouble composing the Großröhrsdorf talk because of conflicting impulses. I had inherited a desire for revenge from my father, who so hated Germany that he volunteered for military service in World War II precisely to go back and kill the people who had murdered his parents. To underline the point, I told them about my parents attending a ceremony in my mother's German hometown but then driving five hours into Switzerland so they would not have to sleep in Germany. As I tried to write the Großröhrsdorf talk, I could feel my father at my side, ordering me not to let the SOBs off lightly.

The desire for revenge had to compete with a powerful longing for reconciliation of more recent vintage. At our community's Holocaust memorial ceremony in 2000, I heard a lecture by Eva Kor, a survivor of the notorious experiments on twins carried out at Auschwitz. She told of the day many years after her release when she was asked to accept an apology from one of the doctors who had been on the camp staff, a man she remembered for his kindness to the victims of these gruesome and sadistic experiments. She talked movingly about how saying a grudging "I forgive you" unleashed a torrent of long-buried feelings. Forgiving this man enabled her to forgive her sister for succumbing to the Auschwitz experiments, her parents for failing to protect her as parents should, and, finally, herself for becoming so deformed by hatred. With Eva's example, how could I refuse reconciliation?

I then read to the Gainesville assembly the text of my Großröhrsdorf lecture from November 7, 2008:

Madame Mayor, members of the Town Council, honored members of my family, ladies and gentlemen:

On the last night of my visit to Großröhrsdorf in 2004, Matthias drove me to the guest house where I was staying. As we said goodbye, he told me solemnly that he knew it was impossible that the Schönwald family could ever return to Großröhrsdorf. But, Matthias said, it was very important that I understand how much the town had lost when the family left Großröhrsdorf in 1939. I believe we hugged and he drove off.

As a result of this week and the efforts that led to it, I think we all know what Großröhrsdorf lost 70 years ago. My family and I are grateful for what you have done to keep alive the memory of the Schönwalds, to honor their legacy, to assemble here tonight to hear from us. My father never returned to Großröhrsdorf, yet here are his children and some of his grandchildren, celebrating and mourning with you.

When I returned home after my first visit to Großröhrsdorf almost ten years ago, I called my brother, eager to tell him the wonderful stories I'd heard about Curt and Regina Schönwald. Almost immediately, we ran into a problem. We had no language to identify the people we were talking about. "Grandfather" and "Grandmother" were titles we had never used for anybody in our lives. Using "Mr. and Mrs. Schönwald" was ridiculously formal, while "Curt and Regina" seemed too intimate for people we had never met. After several pauses, we settled on the awkward phrases "Dad's dad" and "Dad's mom."

As a result of my visits to Großröhrsdorf, Curt and Regina have become my grandparents, not just my father's parents. I have imagined conversations with them, thinking about the wisdom they would have shared, the love they would have expressed, the sense of history and roots they would have imparted. I imagine they would have talked with pleasure about most of their years in Großröhrsdorf, about the friends they made and the acceptance they felt.

Perhaps, too, they would have told me about the dark years after 1935, which is part of their story, too. During these times, they were subject to an economic boycott that forced customers to send their children into the store by a back entrance invisible to the Gestapo cameras set up in the tea shop across the street.[2] The public baths, built with generous contributions from the Schönwalds, posted a sign at the entrance that read "No dogs or Jews allowed." They could have told me as well about the other indignities they experienced, up to and including the mob assault on their shop on Kristallnacht and how they were forced to sell their store at a bargain-basement price to an Aryan businessman. I suspect they would have told me that Großröhrsdorf was like most small German cities during those years, no better but no worse, filled with people who showed them kindness and some who turned their backs.

Getting to know my grandparents as people has been painful. I understand only now what it meant to lose them from my life. In the past, I always knew with my intellect that my father's parents had been murdered, but there was a distance between them and me that made it possible to speak of them almost clinically. Now, because I know Curt and Regina as kind and caring parents, as generous people who loved children, their lives *and* murders are real to me. I grieve for them not as abstractions but as my flesh and blood, family members who had emotions, fears, passions, hopes, and dreams. I am angry that

---

2. I learned from a conversation with Matthias that the cameras belonged to the SA.

I was denied their company in my childhood. In short, I now own the pain that comes from their loss. Strangely, all this makes me very grateful.

My father spent years refusing to seek compensation from the German government. In furious arguments, he told my mother he would never accept what he called "blood money." He felt the debt that he was owed for the murder of his parents could never be paid off, least of all with mere money.

In my mind, whatever debt Großröhrsdorf owed the Schönwald family has now been paid in full. You may be as shocked to hear these words as I am to say them. By all you've done this week and the many weeks before you knew of our existence, you've given us back memories of things we couldn't remember on our own. For that, I consider the books balanced.

With the debt to my family retired, the Schönwalds now belong to Großröhrsdorf, to you. How will you deal with them?

After World War II, the victorious Allies debated whether only Nazi party members or the German people as a whole should be held responsible for World War II and the attempted genocide of the Jewish people. In my household, there was no doubt who was guilty. When I first visited Germany as a student in 1974, my eyes could see only Nazis.

I no longer believe in collective guilt, that people born during or after the Holocaust should somehow be deemed guilty simply because they are Germans. Although I no longer believe in collective guilt, I do believe in collective responsibility. Let me explain the difference.

As an American, I consider myself personally obliged to atone for two great sins in my country's history, the enslavement of black people and the mistreatment of Native Americans. For these people, the guarantees of freedom and opportunity so important in my life were nothing more than a cruel joke. Even though my family was not a party to this oppression, arriving long after the original sins, I consider them part of my legacy as an American. It means I inherit a moral obligation to atone for their mistreatment by ensuring that African-Americans and Native Americans are treated with justice and dignity.

In the same way, I believe, your inheritance as Germans is the Holocaust. It is your birthright. You have responsibilities to this history. So again I ask: How will you deal with the legacy of the Schönwalds, a family that most of you never knew beyond legend or rumor?

I can't tell you what to do because this is something you have to resolve for yourselves. I can only give you choices. I hope at least you'll never forget the damage that results when a person is treated, in Martin Buber's words, as an "it" rather than a "thou." I hope you will think about the strangers who live among you now and deal with them as creatures fashioned in God's image. When you pass the Schönwald store, I hope you explain to your children and grandchildren what happened there and why they must not let it happen again.

When my father became an American citizen in 1943, he changed his name from Heinz Schönwald to Henry Wald. When I later asked him why, he said jokingly that World War II was not a good time to have a German name in America. It never occurred to me to ask him why he chose to drop the first part of the family name – Schön, or "beautiful" in German – and keep the second. After all, "schön" could be rendered in English as the very Anglo-Saxon sounding "shane." Yet he kept only "Wald," the German word for dark forests.

I think my father could not bear a name that associated beauty with Germany, and so he left "Schön" behind in the place where his parents were slaughtered. As you may know, the Nazis required that all Jewish women take the name of "Sarah" on their passports. You might thus imagine that both names, "Sarah" and "Schön," were forever banished from our family history, but that is not so. In an act that reclaimed both names, my brother gave his daughter the first name of Sarah and, for her middle name, the "Schön" that had disappeared from our history in the 1940s. By your actions this week, you have done your part to reconnect our German name with beauty. Please let that spirit guide your actions as we entrust you with the Schönwald legacy."

I was curious and a bit apprehensive about the effect of my lecture on the people of Großröhrsdorf. I had not tried to claim that all was forgiven. Rather than bestow cheap grace on the audience, I emphasized the need for atonement. Yet as much as I was tempted, I did not want to cast indiscriminate blame on the citizens of Großröhrsdorf. By the number of people who approached me with tears in their eyes or hugged me fiercely, I realized how much it meant for them to encounter a living Schönwald.

The immediate effect of the talk in Gainesville was apparent on my daughter's face. The grief, sadness, and tears that poured from her eyes distressed me as a parent and I wanted to comfort her. But I also want to teach the family legacy to my offspring even if it makes them uncomfortable.

And what of reconciliation in Germany itself? As one resident of my grandparents' former home said, gesturing to the monument, it was good to have the Schönwalds back in Großröhrsdorf. There was more. My brother, who had once asked me why I was hanging around a bunch of murderers, had come on the trip only at the urging of his daughter. Anticipating that he would hate the experience, he had scheduled a trip to Israel as an antidote. As we drove to Berlin after the unveiling, he admitted that he wasn't sure that Israel could measure up to the week in Großröhrsdorf. I think that even my father, implacable though he was, might have grudgingly considered the whole affair worthwhile. It might even have made him whole again. I realize, in sum, that a lot more was reconciled that week in Großröhrsdorf than just me.

12 ON STAGE

The three amateur historians from Großröhrsdorf undertook their mission because they believed Germans who had not learned about the Holocaust from the communist rulers of East Germany urgently needed to know it. Norbert, Eckhard, and Matthias felt a special responsibility to rekindle the memory of the family in the small city where the four Schönwalds lived and worked. They became the chief caretakers of the Schönwald legacy.

Almost 5,000 miles away and several years later, a high school teacher developed a parallel sense of mission to publicize my family's German history in Lincoln, where some of the Schönwald family's survivors had settled. Like Norbert in Germany, this young teacher believed that the Holocaust would mean more to his students if it connected to a local family. After learning about my grandparents' letters to my father, he asked if he could draw from them to write a play about the family. The play, which debuted in 2014, has now been performed in several venues and will continue to bring history alive as a resource for Holocaust education. Much as the work of my German friends set into motion a wholly unexpected reconciliation between Großröhrsdorf and me, the play written and first performed in Lincoln brought a sense of healing that I did not know I needed.

I left Lincoln in 1971 to attend graduate school out of state, returning only for short visits to my hometown. As often happens, this distance made me think nostalgically of Lincoln as a place full of gentle Midwesterners who practiced "Nebraska Nice," a good place to raise children. That mindset left little room for critical reflection until I began work on this book.

Growing up there in the 1950s and 1960s, I didn't think of Lincoln as a hotbed of antisemitism or Nazi sympathizers, but the atmosphere became more polluted by those toxic fumes in the 1990s. Cleansing beams of sunlight occasionally pierced the growing clouds of hate, such as when a local cantor and his wife reached out to a Klansman and neo-Nazi who had left them threatening phone messages and hate mail.[1] They eventually met the man, a late-stage diabetic confined to a wheelchair. They took him into their home and nursed him through his illness, and he soon renounced his racism and even converted to Judaism. He is buried in the Jewish section of a local cemetery with a Star of David adorning his headstone.

Lincoln was not entirely innocent of antisemitism during my sojourn there. Before the term Holocaust denier became common, Lincoln was home to one in surgeon Robert C. Olney. Olney was sometimes described as eccentric or controversial but less charitably by others as a crackpot.

Pioneering the doctrine of "alternative facts," he published a letter in the *Lincoln Journal* in 1966 asserting authoritatively but without a shred of evidence that stories about the Nazi death camps "were purely fiction" and that no one was murdered there.[2] The letter agitated my father, who wrote a reply challenging Olney to disprove eyewitness testimony to the contrary by American military leaders such as Gen. Eisenhower and Gen. George C. Patton.[3] The challenge went unanswered.

A long string of incendiary letters to the editor and extremist tracts poured like a noxious oil slick from Olney's pen. He blamed Jews for virtually every social and political development that he disliked, which was pretty much every one of the time. The line between Holocaust denial and antisemitism, noticeably thin at any time, was completely eradicated by Olney's work for the right-wing Committee of the States and his sponsorship of Elizabeth Dilling, a fanatical Nazi sympathizer from Chicago who was indicted for sedition during World War II. Olney created a foundation with himself as president and chief propagandist, promoting Dilling's peculiar theories about the alleged Talmudic origins of communism and its supposed

---

1. Kathryn Watterson, *Not by the Sword: How the Love of a Cantor and His Family Transformed a Klansman* (New York: Simon & Schuster, 1995).
2. Robert C. Olney, "Pharisee Confusion," *Lincoln Journal-Star*, April 17, 1966, 4.
3. Henry W. Wald, "Dilling Literature," *Lincoln Journal-Star*, April 24, 1966, 4.

embrace by Roman Catholics.⁴ She also characterized Gen. Douglas MacArthur – a right winger who lobbied hard to bomb Chinese military forces in Korea, ostensibly with nuclear weapons – as "a servant of the Jews and their communist comrades."

The Anti-Defamation League took notice of Olney, calling him a vulgar antisemite pervaded by a form of neurotic hate "which has been utterly rejected by all decent Americans."⁵ An FBI source who investigated the physician due to his role in various ultra-right segregationist organizations such as the States Rights Party and Freedom Volunteers described him as "an oddball," a gentler term than I would have used.⁶ Although his obituary decorously mentioned his "conservative politics," it omitted any reference to his fervent support for segregationists and antisemites.⁷ He might best be described, as was another activist of equally indiscriminate hatred, as "a whirling dervish of crazy right-wing energy."⁸ As I can recall, Olney was largely discounted outside the local lunatic fringe.

The Olney episode was not the first time my father tried to alert his fellow Americans to the danger of Nazi sympathizers in the United States. I learned this from a declassified 1952 memorandum written by J. Edgar Hoover in response to a letter from US Senator Fred Seaton of Nebraska that involved my father.⁹

My father had called the senator's attention to a letter in *Time* magazine that attempted to exonerate seven Nazi defendants convicted of war crimes by the Nuremberg tribunal. The Nazi defendants, the letter claimed, were "courageous military leaders" and "faithful administrative officials" who were only doing their duty. Their misfortune, which more detached observers described as well-earned punishment for crimes against humanity, "lay merely in being on the losing side."

The author of the letter, H. Keith Thompson, Jr., was a self-described fascist and disgraced Marine dismissed from military service after a court

---

4. Mike Baxter, "Literature of Discord 'Based on Fear,'" *Lincoln Journal-Star*, December 5, 1965, 18D.
5. "Answers from Art," *Jewish Press* [Omaha, NE], April 15, 1966, 5.
6. Internet Archive, compilation of FBI documents at https://archive.org/details/galewilliampottercommitteeofthestatessanfrancisco10063097and100a80325/page/n61/mode/2up, 109.
7. "Services to be Friday," *Lincoln Journal-Star*, April 22, 1982, 22.
8. Scott Seligman, "The Franklin Prophecy," *Tablet*, August 5, 2021, https://www.tabletmag.com/sections/news/articles/franklin-prophecy-seligman
9. Letter from J. Edgar Hoover to Director of Naval Intelligence re H. Keith Thompson, July 1, 1952.

martial for moral turpitude. Hoover's memo referred the matter to Naval Intelligence, which had already investigated Thompson. The voluminous records of the FBI investigations concluded that although Thompson was undoubtedly a neo-Nazi, he was a nuisance rather than a threat to national security. My father thought otherwise.

My father took umbrage at other public statements that seemed to excuse or exonerate Nazis. I remember when he raged against claims by the National Rifle Association (NRA) that Jews could have prevented the Holocaust had they been armed.[10] In a 1968 letter to the local newspaper, he quickly refuted the false assertion that the Nazis' first step in gaining power was confiscating weapons from civilians. Germany, like most of Europe, had regulated gun ownership as early as 1871 and few Germans other than hunters possessed weapons. He accused the NRA of adopting the Nazi technique of the Big Lie, repeating a false statement so often that people would come to believe it.

His comments about the myth were much less restrained at the dinner table. My father emphasized the absurdity of thinking that half a million Jews, making up less than 1 percent of the population, could have mounted an effective armed resistance against the German army, whose 100 thousand soldiers were augmented by more than two million well-armed Nazi paramilitaries when Hitler came to power. He was angry because he recognized this foolish fantasy for what it was – blaming the victims for their own deaths.

After Olney died in 1982, the soiled banner of Nazism in Lincoln was taken up by another strange bigot. In 1995, police in Denmark arrested a Lincoln resident, Gary Lauck, on an Interpol warrant requested by Germany. The FBI and CIA had watched Lauck export pro-Nazi hate propaganda to Germany and elsewhere from his family's home in Lincoln. Although protected in the United States by the First Amendment, Lauck's activity broke numerous German laws. Arrested while visiting Denmark, he was extradited to Germany, tried, and convicted on multiple charges, and sent to prison for four years.

Even with his notoriety, Lauck didn't matter much on the local scene. Derided as the "Farm Belt Führer" for his ridiculous Hitler-style moustache, he was described as a pathetic loser living in his mother's basement, professing love for a German homeland that found him repulsive

---

10. To understand why resistance was virtually impossible in ghettos and concentration camps, for Jews and other prisoners, see Hayes, *Why?*, 176-217.

and banned him from entry. He was an embarrassment rather than a threat and lapsed into obscurity upon his release.

However, perhaps some of his toxins leaked through the basement floorboards and into the soil. On April 20, 1995, the year Lauck began his forced sabbatical in a German prison, three students from Goodrich Middle School disrupted a funeral at the Jewish cemetery in Lincoln by shouting "Heil Hitler" and other Nazi slogans. They spit tobacco on the hallowed ground. After standing menacingly behind the rabbi, showering the attendees with insults, they goose-stepped away as they left the cemetery. My father, mother, and other survivors from our social network are buried in that cemetery.

Although the court ordered the students to apologize to the Jewish community and perform community service, it took nine years before the school atoned for the sin. An administrator familiar with the incident and later assigned to the school recognized the potential for a teachable moment in 2004.[11] To rebuild relations between the Jewish community and the pupils, Tom Kolbe and a sixth-grade teacher assigned students to write biographies of several of the people interred in the cemetery. The students read their profiles at the cemetery to a group of Lincoln Jews. Their research was later recounted in a video they made that included interviews with descendants of Jewish pioneers who had arrived in the city decades earlier.

The teaching assignment appears to have worked for at least one of the students who had desecrated the cemetery. News coverage of the video in 2004 prompted one of the miscreants to write to his old school. He told students he now realized the foolishness of his actions and deeply regretted the pain he caused, cautioning them to remember that their actions would paint images that could never be erased. In a remarkable but perhaps naïve show of idealism, the students dedicated their video to this perpetrator who had recanted his crime.

At that 2004 gathering in the cemetery, Tom learned about my father's wartime experiences from a chance conversation with a leader of the Lincoln Jewish community.[12] Interested in making a personal connection with somebody from Lincoln who had family connections to the Shoah,

---

11. Miriam Colton, "Act of Hatred Becomes a Tool to Teach Tolerance," *Forward*, August 13, 2004.
12. By chance, the person who spoke to Kolbe was the very same man who had first told me the story about my father's interrogation of a German soldier from his hometown.

Tom posted an inquiry in the Survivor Registry at the US Holocaust Museum. I responded by sending him the *Midstream* essay. He sent me the video made by the students two years earlier.

Since I moved away, immigration has transformed Lincoln from a city dominated by whites of mostly Western and Central European ancestry to a much more diverse community. Growing up, I was aware of cultural diversity beyond the Jewish community mostly through the city's small African American and Native American populations. Today, almost one in ten residents is foreign-born, and the nonwhite share of the population has more than quintupled since the 1971 census. The school board now offers its major informational booklet in Arabic, Karen, Russian, Spanish, and Vietnamese as well as English. Lincoln High School, which serves most of the neighborhoods where many recent immigrants live, enrolls students from 49 countries of birth with 42 different home languages. Among other contributions, the immigrants have brought with them cuisines that were not available in restaurants when I lived in Lincoln.

The growing social diversity has generated both generosity of spirit and occasional expressions of hostility. I was writing the first draft of this chapter when I learned that the South Street Temple, a Reform Jewish congregation in Lincoln, had just been defaced by graffiti. The person responsible for the attack painted red swastikas and other anti-Jewish slogans on the front of the ornate building. He was apparently too busy to notice the surveillance cameras that captured his hate crime and led to his arrest. I'm happy that the local police received numerous tips that identified the man, Noah Miller. A spokesperson from the temple kindly observed that the young man needed counseling which I fervently hope he gets – behind bars.

Miller fit the usual profile of Nazi losers, with eight criminal convictions in the three years since he turned 18.[13] For the hate crime against the South Street Temple, he was sentenced to a year in prison. He was soon charged with other crimes, including car theft and passing fake dollars at a fast-food joint.[14] After vandalizing the synagogue, he racked up nine additional charges on various violations. Like an inmate in *The Shawshank Redemption*, Miller was not very good at being a criminal.

---

13. Lori Pilger, "Suspect in Temple Vandalism in Court," *Lincoln Journal Star*, February 25, 2020, A6.
14. Lori Pilger, "Vandalism Suspect Now Faces Other Charges," *Lincoln Journal Star*, January 5, 2021, A5.

Some years after the cemetery vandalism, Tom was having coffee with another teacher from Lincoln High. He mentioned my family's Holocaust connection to Chris Maly, a brilliant and committed teacher of English and drama at the school. Chris had developed innovative ways to teach tolerance to students in his diverse and multicultural classrooms. He won a major award from the National Education Association for a project on Emmett Till, the Black youth from Chicago lynched in Mississippi in 1955.

Excited by the opportunity to connect his teaching to a local family, Chris began (in his own words) cyberstalking me. In his first email, he told me that his grandfather was a liberator in the second world war, a term used to describe soldiers who freed the inmates from concentration camps. He suffered PTSD from the horrors, imbuing Chris with a sense of responsibility to tell the stories of the pain and loss that hatred unleashes. Chris often reminds me of Norbert in his passion for overcoming hate. When he subsequently asked to see my grandparents' letters, the source of my *Midstream* essay, my brother and I met with him and Tom Kolbe during a chance visit to Lincoln. We weren't going to entrust this precious inheritance to just anybody.

We quickly learned that Chris was not just anybody. Satisfied that he meant what he said about respecting the material, we granted him access and he eventually wrote a play based on my article in *Midstream* and the text of the letters. "The Ghosts on the Wall" was first performed at Lincoln High in 2014 in my presence and in an abbreviated form at a TED Talk later that year. In the play, simply but brilliantly staged, my grandparents sat in their Berlin apartment, reading aloud from selected letters they wrote to my father. A uniformed Nazi stalked the stage, reading out directives and anti-Jewish laws, some of which were projected visually on the set. The actor playing me served as the narrator, speaking lines drawn from the essay. My grandparents' attempts to escape Germany were symbolized by a suitcase that was carried back and forth across the stage.

That would have been the end of it except for yet another coincidence. In May 2017, the Actors' Warehouse of Gainesville, where I have lived since 1983, staged *Bad Jews* in its theater. The play involves three 20-something Jewish cousins struggling over possession of a piece of jewelry that their grandfather had hidden during the Holocaust. As a member of the board of the Jewish Council of North Central Florida, I was invited to join a panel discussion after the play. I later chatted with Steven Butler and Robert Sturmer, the leaders of the theater group. They asked if I could suggest other Jewish-themed plays. I sent them Chris's script from the Lincoln High production.

Steven contacted me about a year later to ask if the Jewish Council would be interested in having "Ghosts" performed locally. I suggested that it might be suitable as part of the annual Holocaust Remembrance ceremony that the council sponsored, the event where I spoke in 2009. To keep the event fresh, we had begun to include some performances in the ceremony but had not yet presented a play. The council embraced the idea of partnering with the theater group to present the play in 2019. Actors' Warehouse appointed a director, put together a cast, and adapted the play for a performance at Congregation B'nai Israel, which hosted the annual remembrance ceremony. The director, Chuck Lipsig, had a grandmother who lost family in the Holocaust and was very committed to the project.

Having never put on a play for the annual remembrance, we had no idea if anybody would attend. Thanks to a local television station and a long newspaper story, the play drew an estimated 400, at least twice our normal attendance. We had to open the folding wall between the sanctuary and the social hall to accommodate the crowd. As problems go, it was a nice one to have.

I was even happier when the Actors' Warehouse staged the play for two weeks in its theater in November 2019. Using the group's performance space rather than the modest "stage" at the synagogue, the director was able to add some powerful choreography by having the Nazi official repeatedly invade the space of the Schönwalds, gradually stripping away the furnishings until Curt and Regina were confined to one remaining table on a nearly bare set. The play ran to full houses for ten performances. The COVID-19 pandemic, which prompted the suspension of live theater, gave new life to the play as it was offered online in 2020. There are plans afoot for performances in other Florida cities and to make the play available for Holocaust education in Florida schools. Thinking the time was right, Chris presented the play in a somewhat revised format at Lincoln High in 2021.

Whether sitting in the audience or watching the play on video, I was especially moved by one scene near the end.

Curt and Regina sat side by side at a table in their Berlin apartment, reading aloud from letters they had written to their son in far-off America. The Nazis had quietly stripped away their furnishings, leaving an almost empty stage that communicated how utterly alone they had become. They continued reading the letters, my grandfather mostly describing his efforts to secure visas so they could join Heinz in the United States, my grandmother dispensing motherly counsel and emotional warmth to the young man navigating life in a new country. With my eyes riveted on my grandparents, I almost missed the menacing, black-clad Nazi official slide silently behind them. They startled visibly when he suddenly clamped his hands on their shoulders. Once the shock passed, the married couple looked at one another for a moment, smiled wanly, and stood. They each took hold of one of the suitcases lined up in front of the table and marched stoically off the stage, exiting quietly through a side door.

Bracing though it was, the final scene from the play was a fictional version of my grandparents' 1942 arrest and deportation from Berlin. The real-world version was a nightmare that began with a deportation notice arriving in the mail. As a rule, the government used the softer term "evacuation" as if the recipients were being moved to high ground during a flood, but Jews already knew that it meant transport "to the East" and probable death. The mailing included a 17-page document that instructed the doomed recipients to meticulously inventory their household goods, disclose all their financial assets, and sign a form recognizing "that my entire property and that of my family members is considered confiscated." As for a right of appeal, the document told them that any action against these measures "will be most strictly punished by state police."

After losing their only income-producing asset (the business in Großröhrsdorf) and depleting resources for the almost four years they lived in Berlin, their financial worth amounted to about $15,000, and household goods valued at $1,900 when they were seized. The confiscated money from the banks was divided between the Reich and the local government's office of High Finance. Furniture and other goods were allocated to dealers who, once the evacuation was over on March 28, loaded the property onto vans, sent it to warehouses, and redistributed some of the furnishings to Aryans.[15] Like an organized crime syndicate, the state and the Reich received a cut of the proceeds.

The autopsy of the Schönwalds' finances, a fitting term for this state-mandated plunder, ran to almost 90 pages of dense text.[16] They signed the form on March 12, 1942, submitting to the further indignity of substituting the Nazi-mandated middle names. They were also required to pay their final gas and electric bills on a special "Form for Evacuated Jews" provided by the state. The letters from my father, which I'm sure were packed in their luggage, have never turned up. I don't know how my grandparents

---

15. Adam Sacks, "Can I Have that Vase?" *Jerusalem Report*, April 19, 2004, 46.
16. Chief Treasury Administration, "Schönwald, Curt Bernhard Walter file," reproduction provided by the Brandenburgisches Landeshauptarchiv.

made their way to the gathering place where they would be loaded on trains, but I'm sure it was designed to humiliate them.

Piaski, the "transit ghetto" where my grandparents were initially sent, is more than 800 kilometers [500 miles] from Berlin. The process was described by Polish Holocaust historian Robert Kuwalek in a 2008 letter to Norbert:

> "... the trains with the people who were sent to Piaski were stopped on the railway station in Trawniki and people had to walk to Piaski, a distance about 11 km [seven miles]. For old people and children, there were organized horse wagons on which they were transported to the ghetto. . . [Those who survived their incarceration were eventually sent to death camps.] They had to walk to Trawniki where they were loaded on the trains."[17]

I am not certain of the facts about my grandparents' next journey – from life to death. They may well have succumbed to the emaciation, hunger, and rampant diseases that were commonplace in the ghetto. If they survived that deprivation, they could have been put on several transports of Trawniki inmates to death camps. Or they might have died in a mass killing in Trawniki on November 3, 1943. That atrocity was captured in a chilling account by a reporter for the *Los Angeles Times* in 1985:

> "Jewish prisoners had been forced to dig a network of trenches and then lie down in them, naked. Guards machine-gunned them, a hundred at a time, until thousands filled the earth. Nazis blared music from the camp loudspeakers to drown out the cries all that morning, noon and night. When it was over, up to 10,000 corpses were set ablaze."[18]

The newspaper story recounting the massacre was written to tell of the impending deportation of a Trawniki camp guard who had misrepresented his military background when he immigrated to the United States in 1956.

---

17. Email from Robert Kuwalek to Norbert Littig, August 10, 2008.
18. Richard A. Serrano, "A Nazi's Day of Judgment," *Los Angeles Times*, July 12, 2005, A-1.

Claiming innocence despite his service as a member of the Death's Head Battalion of the SS, the ex-soldier reported he still had nightmares about the massacre that he allegedly was forced to watch as a perimeter guard. I'm sure the handful of survivors of that bloodbath never slept easily either.

Mercifully, I suppose, Kuwalek concluded that my grandparents were probably murdered in Sobibor in 1943. In the death camps, at least, the murderers tried to hide their crimes from the victims.

I knew every line from Chris Maly's play and had written some of the sentences myself, but most of the text was taken verbatim from the letters my grandparents sent to my father. Despite my familiarity with the play's final scene, I always hoped for a different ending. Maybe this time my grandparents would sail to America, reunite with my father, look on approvingly as he married a young Jewish woman who had also fled Germany, and dote on their grandchildren in dignified retirement. Yet no matter how fervently I prayed for a different outcome, they always disappeared from the stage, walking out of my life and into the shadows of the Six Million.

13 AFTERLIFE OF THE HOLOCAUST

I once heard it said that Holocaust survivors lived with packed suitcases under their beds. Their children moved those suitcases into a hall closet, and their grandchildren eventually unpacked them and put the luggage away in the attic. Although metaphorical, the sequence comforted me because it suggested that my children might learn their ancestors' horrific histories without fearing that the same experience would someday ensnare them. Or so I hoped.

Reflecting on the lives of my grandparents and parents, I've been struck by the insidiousness of the Holocaust. Like a poisonous virus, the Shoah seeped into virtually every important life decision my ancestors made – whether and when to leave, where to go, who to seek help from. Though constrained by practical concerns, my life has presented choices that were unavailable to those who experienced the Shoah.

I assumed my children and grandchildren would be even freer than I was to live their lives unfettered by fears related to their Jewish identities. Despite that expectation, I always recognized the need for vigilance in monitoring genocide and embraced the "Never Again!" slogan as a reminder of the ever-present danger. I was not perpetually alarmed by the threats but merely watchful.

In time, I was confident that my children would not have to think about fleeing the land of their birth. Surely, my grandchildren would not need to hear "The Talk" that many Jews of my generation heard from our parents. We were told matter-of-factly, as if discussing gravity or the weather, that some people hated us because we were Jews. Considering us roaches or rats, a few of the most demented antisemites even wanted to exterminate us. In the future, I imagined, our children and certainly our grandchildren would not have to calculate potential risks to their well-being from being recognized as Jews.

It turns out I underestimated the lifespan of the Holocaust. My dream, perhaps better identified as an illusion, was crushed by the Charlottesville (Virginia) "Unite the Right" rally in 2017. Neo-Nazis, gathered ostensibly to prevent the removal of Confederate statues, proceeded to threaten and harass Jews, killed a peaceful protester, and injured dozens more. President Donald Trump asserted there were good people on "both sides" of the controversy. Trump, of course, had been embraced by the alt-right movement, a polite cover for neo-Nazis and fascists of various stripes, and had hired its leading promoter, Steve Bannon, as campaign manager. Trump pointedly refused to condemn movement members or renounce their enthusiastic support. He claimed never to have heard of David Duke, once America's most famous neo-Nazi and later a leader of the Ku Klux Klan.

One of the organizers of the movement, white supremacist Richard Spencer, told his jubilant supporters after Trump's election in 2016 to "party like it's 1933," referring to the year Hitler ascended to office. He led them in chanting "Hail Trump," a variation on the Nazi "Heil Hitler" salute.

Just two months after the Charlottesville rally, Spencer rented the performing arts center at the University of Florida, my home institution for more than 30 years. He announced plans to give a public talk on October 19, 2017. Under state law, the university had to make the facilities available even if the speaker was not sponsored by the university and the message was repugnant to institutional goals. About a dozen of Spencer's minions showed up for the talk, massively outnumbered by raucous protestors. Spencer spent his time on stage whining about the hostile reception from the crowd.

I participated in several meetings before the event and realized that all the institutions involved – the university, local police, state government, city, and county authorities – sympathized with the anti-Nazi protesters even as they protected the constitutional rights of the neo-Nazis. In Gainesville, unlike Germany in 1933 when all such institutions and norms were corrupted by the virus of antisemitism, it was decidedly *not* 1933 again.

Even though the event itself was nonviolent, the aftermath was not. Three of Spencer's supporters from Texas, one of them a twice-convicted felon on parole, drove by a bus stop where several anti-Spencer protesters were sitting. The driver stopped the car and the Spencer acolytes started singing Nazi songs. When the anti-Nazi protestors jeered at them, one of the men got out of the car while the other two urged him to shoot the counter-demonstrators. Exhibiting the same poor judgment that previously had gotten him convicted in Texas, the felon fired a pistol at them. Despite being a Texan, he was just as bad a marksman as he was a criminal. His point-blank shot hit a building behind the bus stop instead of the people he was trying to kill. He was sentenced to 15 years in prison and the driver received five years for his participation.[1]

Although the mobilization against Spencer and the prosecution of the Texans provided some comfort, "The Talk" is still necessary. Indeed, about a year after Spencer's venomous speech, an alt-right activist invaded a Pittsburgh synagogue during Sabbath services and mowed down 11 worshippers while injuring six. It was the worst incident in what had been a violent two years with multiple fatal attacks on Jews and Jewish institutions. The surge in antisemitic attacks coincided with Trump's 2016 candidacy.[2] Then, on January 6, 2021, home-grown Nazis participated prominently in the traitorous insurrection at the Capitol, one wearing a "Camp Auschwitz" T-shirt.

Some might call these outbursts "isolated instances" as if their infrequency should somehow comfort us. But as Armin Rosen pointed out, they are ominous because each incident presents "an instructively terrifying glimpse into a nearby alternate world."[3] For Holocaust survivors and many of their descendants, that alternate world looks a lot like Germany under Nazism.

My fears about antisemitism domestically have since spread to the Middle East, caused by Hamas's wanton, sadistic murders of 1,200 Israelis (and others), widespread rapes of Israeli women, and kidnappings of hundreds more on October 7, 2023. Horrific beyond words, these terrorist attacks ignited a global outpouring of antisemitism where blaming the victim

---

1. Daniel Smithson, "More Prison Time for Driver in White Nationalist Shooting," *Gainesville Sun*, March 18, 2019, https://www.gainesville.com/story/news/crime/2019/03/18/getaway-driver-sentenced-in-shooting-after-richard-spencer-event/5683044007/.
2. Ian Lovett, "Rise in Anti-Semitic Incidents Goes Beyond Recent Violent Attacks," *Wall Street Journal*, December 17, 2019, https://www.wsj.com/articles/rise-in-anti-semitic-incidents-goes-beyond-recent-violent-attacks-11576611407.
3. Armin Rosen, "'Palestinians' Assault Jews Across New York," *Tablet*, May 21, 2021, https://www.tabletmag.com/sections/news/articles/palestinians-assault-jews-across-new-york

became the dominant trope among many protesters. The United States was not spared similar demonstrations by individuals who reflexively held Israel responsible for the deaths of Gazans when Hamas embedded its military resources among the civilian population, including in schools and hospitals. I am struck by how the self-righteousness of many anti-Israel protestors massively outpaces their actual knowledge of the Arab-Israeli conflict in general and the situation in Gaza in particular. Their confidence in the truth of Hamas-provided statistics would be naive if it weren't so infuriating given the history of misinformation flowing from terrorist organizations.[4]

The embrace of the Hamas pogroms and mass murders will pass. I continue to worry mostly about the future of the United States, where my parents obtained sanctuary and the opportunity to restore their lives. The democratic political system and rule of law seem to be hanging by a thread. If that thread breaks, so do our rights to be treated equally as Jewish citizens of the United States. We are not overreacting by interpreting events through the template formed from our ancestors' experiences. History suggests Jews should be more careful than hopeful.

As much as I hope reading about the Schönwalds will promote empathy for the victims of discrimination and encourage less "othering" of those who are not "our kind" of people, I know it's not enough. The limits of empathy were revealed by my mother during my visit to Lincoln in 1980. Although she was generally kind and compassionate, I realized then that growing up as a despised Jew in Germany did not immunize her against the virus of ethnocentrism.

We were watching news coverage of the Mariel boatlift, looking at footage of desperate Cuban émigrés risking their lives on leaky rafts and broken-down boats to reach asylum in the United States. She did not identify with them or see her journey in theirs. Buying into the prevailing moral panic, she told me she worried that "those people" would bring crime and disorder if allowed into the United States. Unknowingly, she used some of the same language and arguments that critics of immigration deployed in the 1940s to keep her, her family, and her husband's parents out of America. If my mother, of all people, could not realize the danger of excluding certain people because they were not "our kind," how could I hope that learning about my family would inspire people without her experience to show kindness to strangers?

---

4. "How the Gaza Ministry of Health Fakes Casualty Numbers," *Tablet*, March 6, 2024, https://www.tabletmag.com/sections/news/articles/how-gaza-health-ministry-fakes-casualty-numbers

I've long recognized the inherent dangers of social identification with any religious, ethnic, or national group. We are social creatures, so group attachment comes naturally. Social scientists have shown how easily members of an in-group can be made to turn against members of virtually any out-group. Although I'm involved in the religious and organizational life of Judaism, I accept my attachment as mostly tribal: Simply put, Jews are my people.

In rational moments, I embrace what I think of as a "gentle" form of tribalism that takes pride in my community but does not require me to reject or deny the rights of other communities to sustain my sense of self-worth. I also recognize that discrimination against one group will inexorably lead to discrimination – and perhaps worse – against other groups. I try to resist it in all forms.

Although it may promote solidarity and fellowship within a social group, experiencing discrimination also can generate bitterness and misanthropy rather than altruism and empathy. Borrowing language from Robert Putnam, we may bond so tightly with members of our own group that we cannot build a bridge to other groups. Some members of disfavored groups may stigmatize so-called undesirables to improve their standing at the expense of others. The advocates of American slavery and segregation exploited that tendency, warning poor whites that Black advances would hurt them.

I can forgive my mother for constraining her empathy for I, too, am sometimes tempted to see another person as an "it" rather than a "thou." As the grandchild of Holocaust victims, I know that kind of thinking took them from me, and I should know better than to propagate it. Yet I have occasionally needed to resist the evolution of my tribalism from a benign sense of fellowship into hostility toward those who are not my people.

The recent outpouring of antisemitism makes me fear that my children or grandchildren may someday need to retrieve the empty luggage from the attic and repack the suitcases that I perhaps naively thought had been safely moved out of sight and mind. My grandparents wished above all else for their children's safety in another country. My parents prayed that my brother and I would never fear for our well-being in the United States. I've hoped since their births that my children and grandchildren would never confront the threat of a reborn fascism. None of us, not my grandparents, my parents nor I, has yet seen our dreams fully realized.

Where can we find safety in a world seemingly gone mad? Could this be the right time for me to accept the passport that the German government has offered to the children of German Jews rendered stateless by the Nazi regime? Irony of ironies, would the same nation that denied passports to my grandparents 80 years ago, consigning them to a brutal death at its hands, now reverse history by offering their descendants shelter and asylum? It speaks to the insidiousness and timeless nature of the Holocaust that I keep that possibility in mind.

We are not done with the Holocaust, and it is not finished with us.

AFTERWORD

Although research for this book exposed me to family tragedies and disappointments, it also eased some pain as I learned more about the lives of my grandparents and parents. Even when my parents were alive, I felt a bit like an orphan, detached from the bustling, pulsating networks of grandparents, aunts, uncles, and cousins of some of my friends. These extended families spoke an exotic language I didn't understand, specifying with lexical precision the proper term for relatives with various degrees of removal and numerical separation. Because the phrase was irrelevant to my life, I never bothered to learn what "second cousin once removed" meant.

My sense of isolation was partially tempered by success in identifying several missing relatives. I was happy to know of Leo Rothschild, Julie Rothschild, and Leonore Glasner, three of the ghosts I resurrected. The discovery was satisfying, but I really wanted access to their memories, to know them as people, as family. It was too late.

Then I stumbled across Ralph Grunewald, my first gateway to living relatives who were eager to talk to me. I was excited, even though I was not sure of the right words to describe how the two of us were related. Even without the proper terminology, I finally found myself with connections to a larger family composed of people invested in our relationship.

The awakening did not stop there. Ralph suggested that I consider having DNA testing, telling me it had alerted him to other family members. Despite deep skepticism about DNA tests to assess ethnicity and nationality, I went ahead. I've since been contacted by two people who are cousins of some sort on my mother's side. One woman had a grandfather who was my grandmother's brother. She told me I matched her DNA profile more closely than all her known cousins. The other contact and I continue to puzzle out the connection documented by our close DNA match. We did meet face-to-face in Melbourne, Australia.

Building these connections made me deliriously happy, even joyful. I was quick to blast out the news to my family. Why have these discoveries raised my spirits so profoundly? In the end, I think I became ecstatic because these new links reminded me that I'm not as alone as I once imagined.

My excitement isn't due solely to a renewed sense of rootedness. The stories are not always heartwarming. The tales are more likely to induce a sigh than a smile, such as when I learned that my maternal grandfather's sister, my great-aunt Julie, was murdered along with her husband in the Lodz ghetto. The Grunewalds lost many more of their clan to the Nazis, and I imagine my newest contacts will tell me about similar catastrophes when we discuss family lineage.

Apart from the personal pleasure of meeting new family members, this ongoing project allows me to fulfill what the philosopher Emil Fackenheim famously called the 614th commandment: "Do not give Hitler a posthumous victory." This decree obliges Jews "to survive as Jews, lest the Jewish people perish. They are commanded to remember the victims of Auschwitz, lest their memory perish. They are forbidden to despair of man and his world, and to escape into either cynicism or otherworldliness, lest they cooperate in delivering the world over to the forces of Auschwitz. Finally, they are forbidden to despair of the God of Israel, lest Judaism perish."[1]

The Nazi Final Solution was not intended merely to exterminate the Jews of Europe and then, in time, the remaining Jews elsewhere. As the bloodthirsty commandant of a concentration camp boasted in *Schindler's List*, the long-term goal was to reduce Jewish existence to a rumor. By forging tighter connections among the remnants of my family, uncovering, saving, and transmitting memories once lost or hidden, I do my best to honor Fackenheim's clarion call. For me, as for Fackenheim, remembrance is an act of resistance.

---

1. Quoted in Robert M. Seltzer, "Judaism According to Emil Fackenheim," *Commentary*, September 1988, 32.

APPENDIX: THE SCRIPT OF GHOSTS ON THE WALL BY CHRISTOPHER MALY

<u>Cast</u>

Ken Wald: grandson, current day

Curt Schönwald: father, Berlin, 1939

Regina Schönwald: mother, Berlin, 1939

Official, Third Reich Government Documents, 1939–1941

Note: This script is a composition of primary source materials written by the listed authors through essays, letters, and government documents.

KEN

I grew up in a house full of ghosts. The spirits were not formless apparitions floating from room to room but strong images in elegantly framed photographs, tethered firmly to the dining room wall by history and memory as much as by wire and hook. This photograph: Posed formally in the fashion of their day, stiff and unsmiling, they did not haunt me. Because of their vast distance from my life, they were my father's parents, not in any sense my grandparents. They were flesh but not blood. All that began to change on a sunny spring afternoon years later as I stood in the kitchen of my Florida home, leafing through a bulging folder rescued from my father's files after his death.

The folder held almost 200 letters and notes his parents had sent from Germany. Faced with a disordered pile of papers written in German, a language I was proud not to read, I sorted idly through the mound of yellowing documents.

I had never asked my father about his parents. My mother had warned me not to open old wounds. Even so, a few things had slipped out over the years.

His parents, Curt and Regina Schönwald, were native-born Germans, descended from a family with Prussian roots going back to the 18th century. A patriotic German, Curt served with distinction in the Kaiser's air force during the First World War, rising to the rank of squad commander (and, it was said, supervising a young pilot named Herman Göring.) After the war, Curt and Regina moved to Großröhrsdorf, a small city just a few kilometers outside Dresden. They were dry goods merchants with a small but prosperous textile store. The only Jews in town, they raised a son, Heinz (my father), and a daughter named Suze. Bar-mitzvahed in the Dresden Synagogue, educated in the local high school, Heinz later attended the Institute of Technology in Dresden and worked in his parents' store.

KEN

Kristallnacht, November 1938. In Großröhrsdorf, the church bells summoned a mob that hurled rocks through the windows of the Kaufhaus Schönwald, the family's department store.

OFFICIAL

Only such measures are to be taken as do not endanger German lives or property... synagogues are to be burned down only where there is no danger of fire in neighboring buildings.

Places of business and apartments belonging to Jews may be destroyed but not looted ...

Particular care is to be taken that non-Jewish businesses are completely protected against damage. Foreign citizens – even if they are Jews – are not to be molested.

On receipt of this telegram, Police will seize all archives to be found in all synagogues and offices of the Jewish communities so as to prevent their destruction during the demonstrations.

KEN

Heinz and Curt were arrested, deported to Buchenwald, and released two months later.

("1939" is projected)
KEN

As the rising tide of antisemitism closed in on the Schönwald family, the first priority was to save the children. My father managed somehow to get out of Germany in 1939, coming to the United States. This began a correspondence of letters you are about to hear from my grandparents to my father. My father is silent; we will never know the words he wrote to them; we will never know the thoughts he had expressed. Just as I never knew in my time with him. Curt and Regina will now speak.

April 5, 1939
CURT

My dear son!

We never expected anything different than you having a tough time at first, but you mustn't lose faith, things will look up soon. When you finally do get something with room for advancement, you will be doubly satisfied. We are especially happy that you are making such advances with the language and that you have no difficulties. I hope that it will stop with mending socks.

REGINA

My dear Henry!

Your lovely letter made us very happy, keep smiling, my dear boy, you didn't go to N.Y. with high hopes after all. You will have to be patient; Rome wasn't built in one day. You can rest assured when it comes to us, we are well, and as soon as the weather improves, I will go for a walk daily with Vatel.

I'm learning to sew with my sewing machine. That's a lot of fun. You will figure out how American English works soon enough. An English accent is not that bad either. There are so many English people in the USA who also talk like that.

Best wishes to you, my dear son.

April 10, 1939
CURT

Mr. Max Haas. This man is a teacher, very religious, so don't mention the fact that you don't believe in it. He is a teacher and once lived here in the neighborhood. Haas supposedly has great connections. Don't call on Saturdays.

OFFICIAL

The emigration of the Jews from Germany is to be furthered by all possible means. The Reich Central office will have the task to devise uniform policies.

REGINA

Do you have bank holidays over there? I would like to correspond with you in English, you must of course write German so that Vatel can read it himself. Father and I take our long walks and we enjoy it very much, we have beautiful spring days. On holidays and Sundays we walk in the forenoon, on other days in the afternoon. Very often we meet Uncle and Aunt and we see the old Berlin – trees and old parks that we knew 35 years ago. Our flat is now very nice and so comfortable.

OFFICIAL

Measures for the preparation of increased immigration of Jews will include the creation of a Jewish organization that can prepare uniform application for emigration.

April 17, 1939
REGINA

Many people have the fortune to reach England these days. How they get there remains unknown. Your description of New York was very interesting. If you have the time, it would be great if you could always write in such detail. We are content like we always were and very happy if we can witness your starting out on your own, a beginning that will hopefully lead to better things.

Have you unpacked your large suitcases yet?

We bought an umbrella for the balcony. We hope to use it often on sunny days.

April 20, 1939 – Hitler's 50th birthday – the largest military parade in Berlin.
OFFICIAL

The Reich stands in the shadow of the German sword. Trade and industry, and cultural and national life flourish under the guarantee of the military forces. ... The name of Herr Hitler is our political program. Imagination and realism are harmoniously combined in the Führer.

April 24, 1939
CURT

Your mother is very worried about you. Keep your chin up high and strive to get ahead. You cannot rely on others to help you out. Always strive for the highest possible goal even if others laugh at you.

May 3, 1939
CURT

I'm sending very special wishes for your birthday because you have to spend it so far away from us. Stay healthy and head towards a bright future.

We will think of you even more than usual on your birthday.

REGINA

I wish you the very best from my heart. Stay healthy and content, then life is bearable. You have come a long way in your life this year compared to 1939. Hopefully this will be the trend for the years to come.

You can imagine how that all makes me feel, but I still am happy about it as well. Is it true that chocolate does not taste very good over there?

May 8, 1939
REGINA

I just read in the newspaper that there will be another ship, and I don't want the opportunity to pass. Vatel is helping with the packing there which should take another few days. I am so delighted with your reports and how your boss has invited you for supper. That shows that he has interest for you and makes me very happy. I wish your father would start learning English. We have renewed our lease for another three years. This apartment can always be rented out if that should become necessary.

Many of the people here are leaving for Cuba these days.

Could you check whether there might be a way for us to make a living over there?

May 23, 1939
CURT

Hans thinks you cannot use the electrical appliances, fan, etc. because of the different type of electricity over there. How is the electricity over there? All of the appliances were adaptable to both types of electricity after all. Apparently, there is a law in preparation which says that parents of non-Americans, as long as they are over 60 years old, can be summoned outside of the quota.

You'll surely find out more about this soon. I will refresh my knowledge of liqueur production again. Do you think this would be useful?

OFFICIAL

Even the migration of only about 100,000 Jews has been sufficient to waken the interest in, if not the understanding of, the Jewish danger in many countries, and it can be foreseen that the Jewish question will develop into an international problem when a larger number of Jews from Germany, Poland, Hungary, and Romania are set in motion by the increasing pressure of their host nations.

REGINA

Your sister Suse will write you before leaving Berlin.

Alfred is making sure that there won't be a tragic scene. We are, of course, witnessing this with one laughing and one crying eye at the same time.

Please write father he should commence to learn English. He puts it off from one week to another and I find he should start now. The evening school is hopefully fun for you. But you have the advantage of speaking the language so well.

I'm glad to hear that your radio is giving you pleasure. I will attend a cooking course next month for fine cuisine. It can't hurt and is the right thing for us women.

A thousand kisses.

May 30, 1939
REGINA

We were at the airport. The farewell scene there is always very short because when they go beyond the barrier we can only see each other. Confronted by this enormous machine, one loses all sense of fear. The plane was Dutch and could carry 18 passengers. They had a 35-minute layover in Amsterdam. Of course, saying farewell was very hard in spite of all the arguments.

A personal question, my dear son, are you keeping your comb and brush clean?

It's great that English has become second nature to you, the faster that happens, the sooner you'll become a perfect Yankee.

OFFICIAL

The Jew has been eliminated from politics and culture, but until 1938 his powerful economic positions in Germany and his tenacious determination to hold out until the return of "better times" remained unbroken.

REGINA

It's pretty hot over here as well. The heat really gets to me when I'm doing my housework. Unfortunately, I'm not losing any weight. Vatel looks better again. His shirts fit him again. Unfortunately, I have so little time for him because of the cooking class, but that will end soon, too. I hope that someday I will get to show you all the things I learned. You are right about getting together with American boys. That is a good idea, I think.

KEN

That was as much of the story as I knew. Of Curt and Regina, I knew only that – to quote my mother's refrain whenever I asked about any of our relatives – "They died in the war." Although nothing was ever said, I understood clearly enough they were not warriors or Resistance fighters, heroic figures firing on Nazi convoys from ambushes, throwing hand grenades during pitched street battles with the SS. In my young mind, if they could not be heroes, they were ... nothing, people defined more by their absence from my life than their presence in another time. As I got older, it became easier to imagine them as a respectable, sedate couple in late middle age, forced into premature retirement by the Nazi seizure of their store in 1939. Bereft of children, isolated, harassed, threatened on a daily basis, it must have felt as if the walls were closing in on them. I pictured them sinking into torpor, surrendering to their ordained fate as Holocaust victims.

June 13, 1939
REGINA

In my class, we made real American sandwiches, but one needs to eat at least two to get full. If you ever find recipes in the newspaper or advertisements with recipes that you could send with one of your letters, I would be very grateful. Are you keeping your comb and brush clean, or do I have to come and check up on you?

July 19, 1939
REGINA

I am participating in a conversational circle which is very interesting. The participants all speak very well, but I think that they have bad pronunciation. We speak only English, translate, debate, and do dictation. I'm not one of the best yet, but maybe that'll change in time.

Margot received her permit for England and will leave with the next children's transport.

July 20, 1939
CURT

We are very agitated right now, and I have to tell you very tragic news. Sadly, builder Brauer died yesterday. It is unbelievable to us that such a righteous man can cease to exist just like that. He died of a middle-ear infection during the operation. I called Dresden yesterday evening after I heard that he was sick and was told the horrible news. Please write immediately to the Brauers, something heart-warming. They were always there for us even during the hardest of times.

August 14, 1939
CURT

As you can see, your parents have excellent intuition, since we suspected that you had lost your job. It wasn't right of you not to tell us about it earlier. Then, we could have discussed the matter. Write to us in detail and keep your chin up, everything will fall in place.

Ok, my son, stay brave and don't let yourself be discouraged. You know my motto, if it doesn't work out the first time, then it will the second or third time, and I hope you will think about my words when things don't go your way.

August 23, 1939
CURT

You look all Americanized, but you seem a little too sad, like when you were a little boy in that one photograph with Suse. Your mother is especially proud of her American. I'm happy to hear that you're stepping into my footsteps with the radio as well. If you like it that much, then you should get yourself a new one. Continue on your path; it is the right one for getting ahead. If you experience a disappointment, nonetheless, don't give up, something will always come along. If you remember this always, then you are just like me. After all the blows that Muttel and I received, nothing worse could happen to us. But we still keep our head up high, especially because we believe in our kids and trust them completely. I hope we will continue to hear good news from you. Nothing could make us more happy than the fact that you are healthy, and that, even if slowly, you are moving ahead.

REGINA

Be patient even if it is difficult for you sometimes. I believe you when you say that you get tired after a day's work. Take care of your feet, that will make standing all day easier.

August 29, 1939
CURT

If you don't hear much from us in the near future, please don't worry about us, we will get through everything.

OFFICIAL

The Tenth Regulation to the Reich Citizenship Law:

The Reich Minister of the Interior may disband Jewish Associations, Organizations, and Institutions ... after the liquidation has been completed the funds will be transferred.

REGINA

Nothing has changed there. Alfred is not doing so well. He really suffers from mood swings. We still have nice, warm days here. I think about you so much, my dear son. The other day it seemed as if you were calling me and I turned around. Maybe it was a psychic connection.

OFFICIAL

Jews may attend only the schools maintained by the Reich.

They are obligated to attend these schools in accordance with the general regulation of compulsory education.

Existing Jewish schools will be disbanded.

October 6, 1939
OFFICIAL

In a speech at the Reichstag in Berlin, Adolf Hitler stated, "What then are the aims of the Reich Government as regards the adjustment of conditions within the territory to the west of the German-Soviet line of demarcation which has been recognized as Germany's sphere of influence? ... An attempt to reach a solution and settlement of the Jewish problem."

October 31, 1939
CURT

Today Mr. Bartenstein left via Italy. Brauers came by last week to say farewell. It was very painful for them and us. It was such a difficult goodbye, as hard as if our own children were leaving. Brauer's friends have made all arrangements and so they left for Chile today.

REGINA

Shorter days are here now, but we get comfortable evenings in exchange.

No. 43,000 is now being called here which will have their turn in the spring. Everything is going faster than expected.

OFFICIAL

Deportation of Jews from Austria to Nisko.

The resettlement operation to Poland will begin at 2200 hours with the first transport of 1,200 Jews fit for work from the Aspang Rail Station in Vienna.

REGINA

We have a telephone now and that is very comfortable. On 11.18, we will celebrate our 30th wedding anniversary and are still happy together and satisfied with each other.

CURT

Since September, the American numbers moved from 43,000 to 47,000. Things are moving fast now.

OFFICIAL

Further transports will leave regularly on Tuesdays and Fridays of each week with 1,000 Jews. The second and third transports will consist of Jews and Jewesses at present under arrest in Vienna.

REGINA

Today was the first really cold day, but we have a nice warm apartment and feel very cozy. So far, we haven't had any snow or ice. Do they celebrate Christmas like they do over here? Are you speaking fluently now?

Do people eat a lot of salads over there? I would like to learn how to make them and also how to make pralinés. Do you think that's a good idea?

January 2, 1940
OFFICIAL

Secret. Instructions for Deportation.

One. Only full Jews will be deported.

Two. The transport leader will be responsible for the assembly, transport, and supervision of his group.

Three. Every transport leader will receive a list at the concentration point.

CURT

I'm glad that you've accepted a job as traveling salesman and have no doubt that you will get ahead with industriousness and perseverance. Just think of me. When I returned from the military and couldn't find a job, I took a job as a traveling salesman selling postcards and going from city to city and worked my way through it. Then, I tried my luck with cigar holders and had a lot of success in my travels. I feel sorry for you and would like to be by your side because I know you and know that this whole thing has got you down quite a bit. But, as I said before, keep your chin up

REGINA

The very best wishes for 1940. You are a Sunday child, and I am absolutely certain that you will continue to have luck. I'm so sorry that you've had to go through so much. I know your nature and can imagine how this would affect you.

I hope it will work out with your new job. You never know what this may be good for. We slept through New Year's, as usual. I heard that somebody is doing great business over there by hand-making pralinés and then selling them. I would really like to learn how to do that, what do you think? If you've taken the salesman job, make sure to wear the proper clothes. You know how important it is to make the right impression when you are trying to sell something.

Is it very cold over there now?

OFFICIAL

Four. The transport leader will inform the officials working with him of names and addresses.

January 16, 1940
CURT

Please make sure to write to us regularly, so that we don't have to wait needlessly, and please write about everything, whatever it may be. Don't lose your courage. Everything will turn out well.

OFFICIAL

Five. Officials appointed for this purpose have received the personal information on the Jews, they will go to the homes of those concerned.

REGINA

We received both of your lovely letters today. You are already in Lincoln for three weeks now and have hopefully found something appropriate. I wish you the best in your new job. I'm glad that things will be easier for you now, and that's how it should be. Start going to church a little more often, people like to see that. You don't have to worry about us. We are healthy and doing well and that is very satisfying.

Are there immigrants there, too?

KEN

In my Holocaust-decimated household, that moment of contact across the generations counted as a family reunion. With a brief message intended only to cheer up her son, Regina dispelled my notion that Curt and Regina had given up on life as the Nazi regime pressed down on them.

As the full set of letters revealed, Curt and Regina did not stop living even as their world turned upside down. Who would have blamed them if they had succumbed to despair as a poisonous set of laws reduced them to servile status?

Within months of Kristallnacht, Jews were banned from sports grounds, public baths, parks, swimming pools, theaters, cinemas, libraries, concerts, exhibitions, and music halls. Soon, they would be ordered to surrender radios, typewriters, telephones, and house pets, forbidden to purchase tobacco or flowers. In a blend of martial law and house arrest that amounted to internal exile, local officials could proscribe Jews from certain areas and order them off the streets at will.

One would not know any of that from the restrained letters sent to Heinz in New York by his parents in Berlin. No doubt mindful of the censor, they betrayed ...

March 21, 1940
CURT

We keep imagining you in your white uniform at the espresso machine. You will hopefully soon get a job that matches your abilities. Could you send us a coffee sample sometime?

REGINA

We have been separated now for one year and I miss you terribly. I hope you brought your winter clothes to Lincoln. It is freezing, and we had a lot of snow. But that's all over now, maybe a nice long summer will follow.

April 5, 1940
CURT

Unfortunately, we will have to think about emigration soon. I forgot to thank you for your congratulations to my 60th, it was a sad day for me without my kids. We want to share in your life as much as possible.

REGINA

The very best wishes for your birthday. Good luck for the coming year. Be a happy and content person. The past 31 years have been nice and happy years for me, and the rest will be even better.

April 19, 1940
CURT

I hope you will still think about us though, because the situation is such that you are our only hope. Otherwise, our life would be meaningless.

OFFICIAL

Those who have been detained should take with them:

a. A suitcase. 50 kg per adult. 30 kg per child.

b. A complete set of clothing.

c. Woolen blanket

d. Food for several days.

e. Utensils

f. Up to 100 Reichsmarks per person.

g. Passports.

April 25, 1940
REGINA

Today, we received a letter from the Brauers. They had some problems with their luggage. They were very happy that you offered to help them. That was the right thing for you to do. That makes a mother's heart beat faster, to know her children are happy is also our happiness.

Thank you so much for your lovely Mother's Day wishes. I will try real hard to make you all proud. You probably knew him. Aunt Markowitz committed suicide ... what a sad affair. I'm learning American English and have to adjust to it quite a bit. But I'm trying real hard to speak it the right way.

June 28, 1940
CURT

As far as I know, our number 55,000 won't be called until spring 1941. I don't want to pressure you in any way, for us to come and join you, but I have to assume that it will possibly be too late already to go over there if we wait until our number is called. That's why I'm asking you to get everything in order as soon as possible. I have heard that if you were to marry an American you would become American within a few months yourself and could then request our immigration outside of the set quotas. I don't know for sure whether this is true. In any case, it would be of advantage to us if we had all of the emigration papers in hand very soon. Of course, I know that you are doing everything in your power for us, and I leave it up to you to do what you can and what you think is right. I will wait for your in-depth account about what you are going to do and how you'll deal with our emigration matter.

OFFICIAL

A questionnaire is to be filled in for every head of family and is to be signed by the official in charge.

REGINA

I was delighted with your lovely lines which gave me so much information. I had already heard about the mentality of Americans. It will be difficult for us, and we will probably always stay the same behind our own four walls. Vatel is learning how to make pralinés and doing well. There's supposed to already be someone in Lincoln who is doing it there and went to the same school as we did.

Our main topics of conversation are always you, our wonderful children. There's four of you now, and I am so happy when I think of you all and how you are mastering your situations. I'm also worried about you, my dear children. It would be too good to be true to think of a reunion, but I still hope for it.

KEN

Curt and Regina betrayed emotion only when their children's welfare was concerned. "I am so happy when I think of you all and how you are mastering your situations," she wrote. "It would be too good to be true to think of a reunion, but I still hope for it." As Curt affirmed, "The only wish your mother and I still have is to be able to be together with you. Hopefully, we will live to see the day."

August 2, 1940
CURT

I'd like to hear what you found out about our emigration situation. We would be grateful if you would do something in that matter. We have been thinking about maybe going to an intermediate country, to Santo Domingo or Shanghai, but in both cases, something has to be arranged from there. I am asking you to please seriously inquire what can be done.

You know I've never put any kind of pressure on you, but now I'm asking you to please do something soon. I'm convinced that you will do anything you can in the matter.

August 9, 1940
CURT

There is a possibility that it may be our turn sooner than in the spring because many people don't have the money for the passage and therefore are not eligible anymore. Additionally, the local consulate is making things more difficult; presently only people that have children over there and vice versa are getting visas, and only if all their papers are in order. We also have to pay a security deposit of $2,000 for both of us because we're not young anymore. Please get in touch with Lothar to settle this.

You can do it much more easily than I can from over here.

Tell him to please pay the deposit in full as he did with you. If he cannot pay the entire sum, we'll have to try our luck with half, but the total amount would be much better.

If anyone gets rejected for any reason, then it becomes much harder the second time around. The situation has changed quite a bit. I'm convinced that you will handle the situation.

I'm starting to master the "th," but otherwise it's difficult to learn English.

<u>August 16, 1940</u>
CURT

The National Refugee Service is in charge of completing affidavits and, after these have been completed and are validated, they secure the fees for passage. Please try to find out what you can. One of the gentlemen lives in Omaha.

The American consulate is denying everything right now and only issues visas in very few of the cases. But we hope that this will change soon because a new consul is arriving soon.

<u>September 3, 1940</u>
CURT

The local consulate is making things incredibly difficult right now. At the moment, only children of Americans are able to get through, and they're greatly reducing the number of immigration cases. I know about a couple whose application was rejected even though their son was making $50 per week. The explanation was that this is not enough money to feed the parents, and also, the son could lose his job anytime.

September 17, 1940
CURT

We're not doing anything about our emigration. We know that you will do everything that's possible. The atmosphere at the local American consulate is totally different now. They're asking totally different questions, some are rather peculiar.

OFFICIAL

Attention should be paid to the following before the apartment is vacated:

a. Livestock and pets are to be handed over.

b. Perishable food stocks are to be collected.

c. Open fires extinguished.

d. Water and gas turned off.

e. Electrical fuses disconnected.

f. Keys are to be tied and labeled.

g. Search for weapons, ammunition, explosives, poisons, and jewelry.

<u>November 1, 1940</u>
CURT

My dear Heinz, I'm quite sure that you have done everything now to have us join you. It must not be possible at the moment. We would live most parsimoniously. The only wish your mother and I still have is to be able to be together with you. Hopefully, we will live to see the day.

<u>November 15, 1940</u>
REGINA

We are reading about snowstorms in the US, did they hit where you are, too? Our life is quiet and the thought of one day being reunited with you gives us hope. A little while ago we celebrated our 31st wedding anniversary. They were good and happy years. Our Vatel is looking as well as he used to, flexible and much younger than 60.

<u>November 29, 1940</u>
CURT

My teacher is very interested and wants to know everything in detail, for example, why a tuxedo is not called "dinner jacket." She thinks that it's a regional dialect or derived from an Indian word.

December 26, 1940
CURT

This is the last letter for 1940 we will send to you. Let's hope that 1941 will turn out to be an easier year for all of us and that your and our wishes will come true.

January 3, 1941
CURT

I hope you had a good New Year's Eve. I also hope that the new year will bring us all good things, especially world peace. We are waiting for that anxiously.

January 10, 1941
CURT

I heard that the regulations at the local consulate have been altered again so that now things will move along a little bit quicker. We hope for the best. You write so nicely about our future reunion and that is a big relief for us because we too have a great desire to come see you as soon as possible. Everything is the same here.

REGINA

We often talk about the time when we're all reunited again and are weaving interesting dreams about it.

OFFICIAL

After the apartment is vacated, it is to be locked and sealed. The keyhole must be covered. The detained will be taken to the bus and handed over to the transport official.

January 17, 1941
CURT

According to the way that numbers are being called here right now, it will be our turn in the second half of this year, in as much as this can be determined. Considerable changes have been implemented at the local consulate that should make getting a visa a bit easier. However, receiving a visa is always dependent on having all papers in good order and being able to verify passage. An affidavit from you is naturally very helpful, even more so if you were married. You can send this paper directly to the consulate and a copy to me. It's a good idea, however, to send any other affidavits, original and copy, directly to me instead of the consulate. There is a particular reason for this which goes back to recent experiences. Once we have these papers, there is still time for the passage. I can send a cable if necessary. A guarantee from Lothar would also be helpful, once I have all papers in hand. I'm convinced that you're doing everything you can to deal with this situation.

REGINA

I can't believe how fast the time passes. We've been living here for almost two years now, a little bit longer than our separation.

January 24, 1941
REGINA

It is difficult to spell all 48 states correctly, but I will try very hard to get them right.

CURT

There are efforts at the American Consulate here to let people skip ahead of their assigned number if all papers are in order. Anton has obtained a visa for his mother for Cuba, and she will leave soon.

January 31, 1941
CURT

The American consulate now announces the numbers publicly and everything moves a lot faster these days. Right now, number 48,300 is being called, but this year, many more will be announced in the second half of the year.

Currently, the consulate values affidavits from married sons more, but there's nothing we can do about that. At the moment, approximately 30 visas per day are issued and only in cases where all of the paperwork is in order and passage can be guaranteed.

REGINA

My dear son, don't worry about our future. Both father and I are in such good shape health-wise that we can surely still earn some money. It's important to know the language. I heard that women can find good jobs as housekeepers even on an hourly basis. That wouldn't be too difficult for me because I'm used to that kind of work. I'm not too worried about such things.

February 21, 1941
CURT

I'm hearing from acquaintances that the consulate now really places importance on the deposit. Once they reject you, it's really difficult to get another chance. The main thing is to get the papers as soon as possible in order to make everything happen. I'm convinced that you're doing all you can. I hope to pay for the passage from here. I will get an approval here for the money.

March 3, 1941
CURT

People have been strongly suggesting that I have all originals of papers because the consulate will work quicker if I hand in everything myself instead of routing it through Washington. The consulate lets a lot of time pass in such cases before one gets a notice that the papers have arrived. When you emigrated, everything was handled completely differently, but you can believe me that I'm well informed. The passage for us can be arranged from here and you won't have to worry about it.

March 6, 1941
REGINA

Do you think it's a good idea for us to learn how to play bridge?

OFFICIAL

It was inevitable that some souls could not face this trial. There were several cases of suicide and attempted suicide in the course of the first hours. Of 2,500 deportees, ten cases. These cases of suicide – there were others during the journey – involved almost exclusively Jews who had moved far from Judaism, had left the community, or were baptized.

June 2, 1941
CURT

There is not much news to report, at least nothing that interests us. We always write if something comes up that would be of interest to you. Is something wrong? It's June now and the papers are still not complete, and the deposit is also still outstanding. I beg you to speed things up a bit and can only repeat that I don't want to push you, but the situation is becoming very urgent.

REGINA

The Plockis were rejected again, we heard, which makes us very sad. We have our nice balcony and enjoy the warm air.

July 16, 1941
CURT

Our emigration issue has changed completely now that the consulates are all closed. It isn't clear at the moment what one should do. Everybody is telling us something different. We have heard that parents' requests are supposedly still possible but only through Washington. We don't know whether this is true. The only possible way now is through Cuba, but this is impossible because of the high deposit there.

OFFICIAL

The situation of the Jews in Germany in summer 1941.

At present the number of Jews taken for labor service in Berlin is approximately 26,000: 55 percent male. Those employed are men aged 14–60 and women aged 16–50.

July 29, 1941
CURT

I know your mood and despair when something goes wrong for you, but I'm asking you to keep a cool head nonetheless. It was Muttel's birthday yesterday, and we thought of you a lot. You can rest assured that I don't blame you at all for this first failure in securing our move. I know for sure and am convinced that you did everything you could. So, I'm asking you to keep your chin up. If something is beyond possible reality then no one can change that. It would be nice if we could still be with you in the near future and not give up hope.

REGINA

I'm sorry to hear that you are worried and sad. My dear son, how could you possibly have thoughts that we think of you as a bad son? On the contrary, we are happy and proud of the love you show us and all the things you would have done if you had been able to.

August 18, 1941
CURT

Unfortunately, we read that our chances for relocation are slim. We are still going to continue to hope for the best.

REGINA

We know very well that you are doing all you can in this matter and are patiently awaiting any new developments. If it should still all work out, then great, but if not, we will have to be patient a little longer. Many parents are sharing our fate. We all have to wait together.

September 4, 1941
CURT

We can't fight the facts and simply have to deal with things as they are. There's no sense in crying about it, that won't change anything and just depresses everybody involved. After all the suffering we've been through and have overcome, we will also be able to handle anything else that may come our way, with the hope that there is still a possibility for us to be united.

REGINA

It is only natural for us to deal with the facts. We have always believed that to cry about things after they're done makes no sense. We are grateful that you've gotten on so well over there and that you are doing fine. We have our hope for a reunion and that is a nice feeling, too.

<u>September 15, 1941</u>
CURT

We have found a cheaper way to go through Cuba. You can see how urgent the situation is for us by the 200 DM [German marks] that I have sacrificed for the cable. I hope we'll soon have better news. Don't use my first name on the cable address to save you money. Together it will cost $2,300, which is a lot cheaper than was the case so far. I will be able to pay for the passage from here. We are healthy.

(Projected cable messages:)

1941 SEP 15 PM 9 24

WMA 421 VIA RCA=CD BERLIN 5075 41 15

$3.61 NLT WALD=

311 NORTH 18 ST. LINCOLN NEBR=

OBTAIN CUBA TOURIST VISA AS SOON AS POSSIBLE VIA IGNATZ ROSENAK 333 BROADWAY NEW YORK TOTAL COSTS 1150 DOLLARS PER PERSON BORROW MISSING MONEY FROM DAN HILL ARRANGE FOR HANS GOSSMAN TO IMMEDIATELY DO ALL NECESSARY THINGS AND FIND OUT WHETHER RESPONSIBLE=

HAPAG

WESTERN UNION

1941 SEP 17 PM 5 27

WMA 311 VIA RCA=CD BERLIN 23/24 17

RP $3.61 NLT WALD=

311 NORTH 18 ST. LINCOLN NEBR=

YOUR LETTER 119 CUBA VISA NOW ISSUED BY CUBA LEGATION

BERLIN AS SOON AS CUBA GOVERNMENT ISSUES ENTRY PERMIT VIA

KABEL=HAPAG

KEN

For almost two years, they explored every potential lifeline no matter how remote it seemed. Although Shanghai, Santo Domingo, and Africa were explored as possible destinations, the Schönwalds concentrated on obtaining visas to join their son in the United States and thus entered a labyrinthine American immigration process made even more feckless by the war. They became subject to a world where something as trivial as a delay in mailing a package or a misplaced signature could set the process back by months or years.

<u>September 29, 1941</u>
CURT

I already struggled with my bad conscience that you may get yourself into deep financial troubles in order to help us. I'm completely convinced that you have tried everything, and it is sad that no success could be achieved. Now, my dear son, I beg you not to be sad because of the failures so far. Someday, everything will work out. You will pay close attention and go after every opportunity that presents itself, I am sure. I will continue to look for opportunities which seem favorable to our relocation.

VOICE

Secret. The emigration of Jews is to be prevented, taking effect immediately.

REGINA

Don't be sad that you weren't able to come up with what you needed. We are healthy, which is the most important thing. We have a few very nice ladies living in our apartment house. We see them often and we all share the same goal, to be with our children. We're having very cool, autumn-like days now, and soon winter will arrive. How is the weather over there right now? Now, my dear, don't get discouraged, with time comes new opportunities.

OFFICIAL

I request that the internal German Authorities concerned in the area of service there may be informed of this order. Permission for the emigration of individual Jews can only be approved in single very special cases; for instance, in the event of a genuine interest on the part of the Reich, and then only after a prior decision has been obtained from the Reich Security Main Office.

<u>October 10, 1941</u>
CURT

This all may sound egotistical, but you can believe me when I tell you that our move has reached a point where every day could make a difference. Everything is very important and urgent now. I'm going with a transit through Spain, maybe even Ecuador. This may cost $500 per person. Will you be able to come up with that much? The money is not lost.

Try everything, dear Heinz, things must move swiftly now, otherwise all opportunities to come join you will be gone.

We are very worried about our move.

REGINA

You are facing new opportunities now, and we are waiting anxiously to hear how things will develop. We heard from Hugo Gossmann's sisters that Aunt Betty is not very happy with you. You supposedly didn't say goodbye to them when you left New York. Is that true?

(Projected cables:)

1941 OCT. 27 PM 5 56

CA 190 VIA RCA=CD BERLIN 26 27

NLT $2.99 HENRY WALD=

LINCOLN NEBR=

WHEN CUBA VISA ISSUED PASSAGE WILL DEFINITELY BE PAID HERE

WAITING URGENTLY FOR REPLY CABLE TO CURT SCHÖNWALD THAT CUBA PAID= ITAL CIT.

1941 OCT. 17 PM 10 08

WMA 432 CABLE=CD BERLIN 60/58

RP $3.16 NLT HENRY WALD=

1320 GSTREET LINCOLN NEBR=

EMIGRATION SCHÖNWALD URGENTLY NECESSARY TRY AGAIN TO GET MONEY FOR CUBA VISA CONSULT FOR IMMEDIATE REALIZATION RICHARD AUERBACH 139 PAYSON AVE NEW YORK COST 1050 DOLLARS PER PERSON STOP SUBMIT ALSO LIEN WASHINGTON REQUEST VISA

AUTHORIZATION FOR AMERICAN CONSULATE MADRID STOP CABLED HANS FOR HELP IN MATTER URGENTLY CUBA IS FASTEST IF IN NEED OF MONEY SELL LIFE INSURANCE CABLE BACK=HAPAG

KEN

They never boarded a ship. They began to explore a more complicated plan involving a tourist visa to Cuba. About seven months later, on November 22, 1941, Curt wrote with the good news. Thanks to Heinz's hard work, they had secured immigration authorization to Cuba, a way station before their eventual landing in the United States. As soon as their new passports arrived, they would book passage. A worried Heinz could now finally relax and accept his father's heartfelt thanks for all his sacrifices. It looked as though the story would have a happy ending.

OFFICIAL

It is intended not to evacuate Jews of more than 65 years of age but to send them to an old-age ghetto. Next to these age groups, of the 280,000 Jews still in Germany proper and Austria on 31 October 1941, approximately 30 percent are over 65; Jews disabled on active duty and Jews with war decorations (Iron Cross I) will be accepted in the Jewish old-age ghettos. Through such an expedient solution, the numerous interventions will be eliminated with one blow.

<u>November 22, 1941</u>
CURT

As soon as we get our passports here we can get our ship tickets. We are waiting every day for the passports and are disappointed about the apparent delay.

OFFICIAL

The carrying out of each single evacuation project of a larger extent will start at a time to be determined chiefly by the military development. Regarding the handling of the Final Solution in the European territories occupied and influenced by us, it was suggested that the competent officials of the Foreign Office working on these questions confer with the competent "Referenten" from the Security Police and the SD [*Sicherheitsdienst*, or intelligence agency]. Certain preparatory measures incidental to the carrying out of the Final Solution ought to be initiated immediately in the very territories under discussion, in which process, however, alarming the population must be avoided.

REGINA

I was very happy to receive your lovely letter and to hear that your boss was nice enough to offer you the loan for the money. This made me especially happy because it shows that he has trust in you. Since you cannot do much about it either way, you'll have to let the cards fall as they may. Please don't forget to say hello to your sister from us all. I beg you from the bottom of my heart, my dear boy, write to her often and stay in contact with her.

My warmest regards and kisses from the bottom of my heart, stay healthy, take care, your Muttel. (SILENCE)

KEN

As far as I know, that was the last communication Heinz ever received from his parents. The Reich had stopped issuing passports to Jews, reflecting the 1941 change in policy from expulsion to extermination. For a brief time, Curt was ordered to work as a slave laborer in a Berlin electrical factory. A Gestapo memorandum dated March 28, 1942, reports that Curt and Regina Schönwald (nos. 10326 and 10327, respectively) were transported by train to Trawniki labor camp near Lublin in Poland. The *Gedenkebuch*, a postwar archive compiled to document the fate of German Jews under National Socialism, confirms the transport but is silent about what happened next to my father's parents. The *Encyclopedia of the Holocaust* notes that many Trawniki inmates died of starvation and disease while others were sent to the Belzec death camp for extermination. Possibly, they were among the 10,000 Jewish inmates of Trawniki shot on November 5, 1943, following an uprising in the Sobibor camp. For bureaucratic reasons, Curt and Regina's official date of death was May 12, 1945, the day the war ended – and Heinz's birthday. Perhaps to rid himself of his ghosts, he insisted that I become a bar mitzvah on the very same day 17 years later.

Through these letters, those ghosts in the photographs that hung on the wall of my childhood home have shed their spectral cloak and assumed human dimensions. Curt and Regina have reached out to me across time, space, and memory. But the most important thing I've learned is that the Schönwalds did not surrender in the face of crushing reality. They did not join the Resistance, but Curt and Regina resisted by refusing to shout lamentations or succumb to despair, by the heroic act of imagining and planning a life for themselves in the New World. My grandparents never got the chance to live that life, except vicariously, but the vision sustained them in the darkest moments. I was wrong when I assumed they were led meekly as sheep to the slaughter. I know now that my mother was wrong when she said they "died in the war." As I learned from their testament, my grandparents died fighting the war.

ACKNOWLEDGMENTS

This book describes my family's Holocaust history, leaving me with numerous debts to the many people who guided my journey. I've tried to recognize the contributors who were essential to the story and ask forgiveness from those I have not mentioned by name.

Several residents of Großröhrsdorf enabled me to get to know my grandparents well enough to write the book. Norbert Littig, Eckhard Hennig, and Matthias Mieth became friends as well as benefactors, turning my interest in the Schönwald family into a passion equal to their own. During visits to Großröhrsdorf, I was able to communicate with my newfound friends thanks to the translation services of Anette Bliss and Kerstin Schneider. Markus Nitsche's late grandfather, a friend of both my father and grandfather, would have been proud of his grandson for welcoming our family back to Großröhrsdorf. The apology from Mayor Kristen Ternes was a moving experience that facilitated a reconciliation with the German people.

Several people from my mother's hometown told me about the history of the Rothschild family in Öhringen. They include Joachim S. Hahn, Walter Meister, Eva and Frieder Diem, and the Förnzler family. Along with other residents, they featured my family during their commemoration of Kristallnacht in 2023 and continue efforts to restore the synagogue that both of my grandparents led.

Schooled in academic writing, I had to learn how to sustain a narrative arc and when to allow my voice into the story without making this a "look at me" book. To the extent I succeeded, it is mostly because two friends and talented journalists, Lynda Schuster and Stacey Goldring, gave me honest, straightforward criticisms that helped improve the manuscript. I'm also grateful for the writing workshop and book conference that Stacey organized in Jacksonville through the "Searching for Identity" foundation. Members of the memoir-writing "pod" sponsored by the Writers Alliance of Gainesville, Alycin Hayes and Elsie Wilson, offered feedback and useful advice as well as compassion and insight.

Chris Maly's transformation of my grandparents' letters into a compelling play script has been equally important to this effort of remembrance. His play has done much to help students imagine the unimaginable Holocaust. Every student should have a teacher like Chris. Steven Butler and the staff of the Actors Warehouse in Gainesville brought the play to life with care and imagination.

I drew heavily from various archives, benefiting from the dogged work and kindness of librarians at several institutions. This included the Nebraska Jewish Historical Society (Kathy Weiner and Renee Corcoran), the Lincoln Public Libraries, the *Omaha Jewish Press* (Annette van de Kamp-Wright), Stanford University Special Collections (Barry Hinman), and the College of Business at the University of Nebraska-Lincoln (Mary Ellen Ducey). Staff members at the US National Archives in Washington, DC; College Park, Maryland; and Kansas City led me to valuable information I could not have discovered on my own.

Librarians at the University of Florida's Price Library of Judaica – Rebecca J. W. Jefferson, Katalin Rac, and the late Emily Madden – found the most obscure documents that I needed when I needed them. My thanks and gratitude to them. Without the extraordinary resources of Ancestry.com, JewishGen, Family Search, and other websites, I wouldn't have learned many things that mattered to the story.

The bulk of translation was ably handled by three students from the University of Florida: Margarit Grieb, Will Lehmann, and Lea Klenke. I also imposed occasionally on German-speaking friends Leah Hochman, Geoffrey Giles, and David Denslow. Thanks for your willingness to be exploited in a worthy cause.

For helping me navigate trade publishing, I thank Susan Ginsburg, John Schline, Sam Freedman and Tom Levenson.

I am honored that the book bears the imprint of Amsterdam Publishers, a company with a mission to counter antisemitism and Holocaust denial. Liesbeth Heenk embraced the manuscript, offered good advice, and husbanded it through the publishing process. The manuscript editor, Larry Hanover, tightened up the text with tact and respect for my intentions.

Thanks to Dara and Jaina, my remarkable daughters, for enriching my life and helping with the book. I'm extremely grateful to my brother's children, Sarah and Aaron, who encouraged me to undertake this memoir.

My youngest daughter once said that (gentle) mocking is an art form in the Wald family and you had better be good at it. In that spirit, I cherished the opportunity to tease my big brother at various points in the text, even if only posthumously. I can almost hear him giving me back more grief than I gave him. Steve's late wife, Linda, was a kind of big sister to me and I miss her dearly.

I am pleased to dedicate this volume to my wife, Robin Lea West. She experienced much of the research process firsthand, helped jog my memory at crucial times, and offered thoughtful criticisms of the ideas I shared and the pages I wrote. Her encouragement, support, love, and dedication were so important in making this volume a reality.

PHOTOS

Regina Schoenwald, date unknown

The Kaufhaus Schoenwald store, 1928

Curt with children on holiday

Ruth, Louis and Margarete Rothschild in garden in Ohringen, early-1930s

Victims of pogrom Oehringen, 1933

Ad for Nazi concerts in Großröhrsdorf, 1933

Advertisement for Schoenwald Store

Announcement of new Kaufhaus Seifert, December 1, 1938

ID photo of Curt Schoenwald as slave laborer, circa 1941

Gretl and Ruth at Tamiment, 1941

Walds in Lincoln, early-1950s

Gretl in US

Henry and Gretl wedding portrait, 1940

Henry in the Army, circa 1941

Hermann Förnzler, mid-1970s

Eckhard Hennig, 2006

Meeting with informants in Großröhrsdorf, 2006

Walds at Schoenwald Exhibition 2008. From left to right: Robin West, Ken Wald, Jaina Wald, Sarah Wald, Steven Wald

Matthias Mieth (left) & Ken Wald at memorial unveiling, 2008

Norbert Littig at Großröhrsdorf talk on November 7, 2008

Monument with Store Reflection, 2008

ABOUT THE AUTHOR

The son of Holocaust survivors and grandson of Holocaust victims, Kenneth D. Wald served six years as director of the Center for Jewish Studies at the University of Florida. He spent four years on the state of Florida's Task Force on Holocaust Education and co-founded and directed the Summer Holocaust Institute for Florida Teachers. In 2011, he was named the University of Florida Teacher-Scholar of the Year, the highest honor given to a faculty member. His most recent book, *The Foundations of American Jewish Liberalism*, won the 2020 National Jewish Book Award.

AMSTERDAM PUBLISHERS HOLOCAUST LIBRARY

The series **Holocaust Survivor Memoirs World War II** consists of the following autobiographies of survivors:

Outcry. Holocaust Memoirs, by Manny Steinberg

Hank Brodt Holocaust Memoirs. A Candle and a Promise, by Deborah Donnelly

The Dead Years. Holocaust Memoirs, by Joseph Schupack

Rescued from the Ashes. The Diary of Leokadia Schmidt, Survivor of the Warsaw Ghetto, by Leokadia Schmidt

My Lvov. Holocaust Memoir of a twelve-year-old Girl, by Janina Hescheles

Remembering Ravensbrück. From Holocaust to Healing, by Natalie Hess

Wolf. A Story of Hate, by Zeev Scheinwald with Ella Scheinwald

Save my Children. An Astonishing Tale of Survival and its Unlikely Hero, by Leon Kleiner with Edwin Stepp

Holocaust Memoirs of a Bergen-Belsen Survivor & Classmate of Anne Frank, by Nanette Blitz Konig

Defiant German - Defiant Jew. A Holocaust Memoir from inside the Third Reich, by Walter Leopold with Les Leopold

In a Land of Forest and Darkness. The Holocaust Story of two Jewish Partisans, by Sara Lustigman Omelinski

Holocaust Memories. Annihilation and Survival in Slovakia, by Paul Davidovits

From Auschwitz with Love. The Inspiring Memoir of Two Sisters' Survival, Devotion and Triumph Told by Manci Grunberger Beran & Ruth Grunberger Mermelstein, by Daniel Seymour

Remetz. Resistance Fighter and Survivor of the Warsaw Ghetto, by Jan Yohay Remetz

My March Through Hell. A Young Girl's Terrifying Journey to Survival, by Halina Kleiner with Edwin Stepp

Roman's Journey, by Roman Halter

Beyond Borders. Escaping the Holocaust and Fighting the Nazis. 1938-1948, by Rudi Haymann

The Engineers. A memoir of survival through World War II in Poland and Hungary, by Henry Reiss

Spark of Hope. An Autobiography, by Luba Wrobel Goldberg

Footnote to History. From Hungary to America. The Memoir of a Holocaust Survivor, by Andrew Laszlo

The Courtyard. A memoir, by Ben Parket and Alexa Morris

Run, Mendel Run, by Milton H. Schwartz

The series **Holocaust Survivor True Stories**
consists of the following biographies:

Among the Reeds. The true story of how a family survived the Holocaust, by Tammy Bottner

A Holocaust Memoir of Love & Resilience. Mama's Survival from Lithuania to America, by Ettie Zilber

Living among the Dead. My Grandmother's Holocaust Survival Story of Love and Strength, by Adena Bernstein Astrowsky

Heart Songs. A Holocaust Memoir, by Barbara Gilford

Shoes of the Shoah. The Tomorrow of Yesterday, by Dorothy Pierce

Hidden in Berlin. A Holocaust Memoir, by Evelyn Joseph Grossman

Separated Together. The Incredible True WWII Story of Soulmates Stranded an Ocean Apart, by Kenneth P. Price, Ph.D.

The Man Across the River. The incredible story of one man's will to survive the Holocaust, by Zvi Wiesenfeld

If Anyone Calls, Tell Them I Died. A Memoir, by Emanuel (Manu) Rosen

The House on Thrömerstrasse. A Story of Rebirth and Renewal in the Wake of the Holocaust, by Ron Vincent

Dancing with my Father. His hidden past. Her quest for truth. How Nazi Vienna shaped a family's identity, by Jo Sorochinsky

The Story Keeper. Weaving the Threads of Time and Memory - A Memoir, by Fred Feldman

Krisia's Silence. The Girl who was not on Schindler's List, by Ronny Hein

Defying Death on the Danube. A Holocaust Survival Story, by Debbie J. Callahan with Henry Stern

A Doorway to Heroism. A decorated German-Jewish Soldier who became an American Hero, by W.Jack Romberg

The Shoemaker's Son. The Life of a Holocaust Resister, by Laura Beth Bakst

The Redhead of Auschwitz. A True Story, by Nechama Birnbaum

Land of Many Bridges. My Father's Story, by Bela Ruth Samuel Tenenholtz

Creating Beauty from the Abyss. The Amazing Story of Sam Herciger, Auschwitz Survivor and Artist, by Lesley Ann Richardson

On Sunny Days We Sang. A Holocaust Story of Survival and Resilience, by Jeannette Grunhaus de Gelman

Painful Joy. A Holocaust Family Memoir, by Max J. Friedman

I Give You My Heart. A True Story of Courage and Survival, by Wendy Holden

In the Time of Madmen, by Mark A. Prelas

Monsters and Miracles. Horror, Heroes and the Holocaust, by Ira Wesley Kitmacher

Flower of Vlora. Growing up Jewish in Communist Albania, by Anna Kohen

Aftermath: Coming of Age on Three Continents. A Memoir, by Annette Libeskind Berkovits

Not a real Enemy. The True Story of a Hungarian Jewish Man's Fight for Freedom, by Robert Wolf

Zaidy's War. Four Armies, Three Continents, Two Brothers. One Man's Impossible Story of Endurance, by Martin Bodek

The Glassmaker's Son. Looking for the World my Father left behind in Nazi Germany, by Peter Kupfer

The Apprentice of Buchenwald. The True Story of the Teenage Boy Who Sabotaged Hitler's War Machine, by Oren Schneider

Good for a Single Journey, by Helen Joyce

Burying the Ghosts. She escaped Nazi Germany only to have her life torn apart by the woman she saved from the camps: her mother, by Sonia Case

American Wolf. From Nazi Refugee to American Spy. A True Story, by Audrey Birnbaum

Bipolar Refugee. A Saga of Survival and Resilience, by Peter Wiesner

In the Wake of Madness. My Family's Escape from the Nazis, by Bettie Lennett Denny

Before the Beginning and After the End, by Hymie Anisman

I Will Give Them an Everlasting Name. Jacksonville's Stories of the Holocaust, by Samuel Cox

Hiding in Holland. A Resistance Memoir, by Shulamit Reinharz

The Ghosts on the Wall. A Grandson's Memoir of the Holocaust, by Kenneth D. Wald

The series **Jewish Children in the Holocaust** consists of the following autobiographies of Jewish children hidden during WWII in the Netherlands:

Searching for Home. The Impact of WWII on a Hidden Child, by Joseph Gosler

Sounds from Silence. Reflections of a Child Holocaust Survivor, Psychiatrist and Teacher, by Robert Krell

Sabine's Odyssey. A Hidden Child and her Dutch Rescuers, by Agnes Schipper

The Journey of a Hidden Child, by Harry Pila and Robin Black

The series **New Jewish Fiction** consists of the following novels, written by Jewish authors. All novels are set in the time during or after the Holocaust.

The Corset Maker. A Novel, by Annette Libeskind Berkovits

Escaping the Whale. The Holocaust is over. But is it ever over for the next generation? by Ruth Rotkowitz

When the Music Stopped. Willy Rosen's Holocaust, by Casey Hayes

Hands of Gold. One Man's Quest to Find the Silver Lining in Misfortune, by Roni Robbins

The Girl Who Counted Numbers. A Novel, by Roslyn Bernstein

There was a garden in Nuremberg. A Novel, by Navina Michal Clemerson

The Butterfly and the Axe, by Omer Bartov

To Live Another Day. A Novel, by Elizabeth Rosenberg

A Worthy Life. Based on a True Story, by Dahlia Moore

The Right to Happiness. After all they went through. Stories, by Helen Schary Motro

To Love Another Day. A Novel, by Elizabeth Rosenberg

The series **Holocaust Heritage** consists of the following memoirs by 2G:

The Cello Still Sings. A Generational Story of the Holocaust and of the Transformative Power of Music, by Janet Horvath

The Fire and the Bonfire. A Journey into Memory, by Ardyn Halter

The Silk Factory: Finding Threads of My Family's True Holocaust Story, by Michael Hickins

Winter Light. The Memoir of a Child of Holocaust Survivors, by Grace Feuerverger

Out from the Shadows. Growing up with Holocaust Survivor Parents, by Willie Handler

Stumbling Stones, by Joanna Rosenthall

The Unspeakable. Breaking decades of family silence surrounding the Holocaust, by Nicola Hanefeld

Hidden in Plain Sight. A Journey into Memory and Place, by Julie Brill

Untold. From Austria to America and Back, by Anne Hand

The series **Holocaust Books for Young Adults** consists of the following novels, based on true stories:

The Boy behind the Door. How Salomon Kool Escaped the Nazis. Inspired by a True Story, by David Tabatsky

Running for Shelter. A True Story, by Suzette Sheft

The Precious Few. An Inspirational Saga of Courage based on True Stories, by David Twain with Art Twain

Dark Shadows Hover, by Jordan Steven Sher

The Sun will Shine on You again one Day, by Cynthia Monsour

The series **WWII Historical Fiction** consists of the following novels, some of which are based on true stories:

Mendelevski's Box. A Heartwarming and Heartbreaking Jewish Survivor's Story, by Roger Swindells

A Quiet Genocide. The Untold Holocaust of Disabled Children in WWII Germany, by Glenn Bryant

The Knife-Edge Path, by Patrick T. Leahy

Brave Face. The Inspiring WWII Memoir of a Dutch/German Child, by I. Caroline Crocker and Meta A. Evenbly

When We Had Wings. The Gripping Story of an Orphan in Janusz Korczak's Orphanage. A Historical Novel, by Tami Shem-Tov

Jacob's Courage. Romance and Survival amidst the Horrors of War, by Charles S. Weinblatt

A Semblance of Justice. Based on true Holocaust experiences, by Wolf Holles

Under the Pink Triangle, by Katie Moore

Amsterdam Publishers Newsletter

Subscribe to our Newsletter by selecting the menu at the top (right) of **amsterdampublishers.com** or scan the QR-code below.

Receive a variety of content such as:

- A welcome message by the founder
- Free Holocaust memoirs
- Book recommendations
- News about upcoming releases
- Chance to become an AP Reviewer.

www.ingramcontent.com/pod-product-compliance
Lightning Source LLC
LaVergne TN
LVHW041928070526
838199LV00051BA/2745